Acclaim for Beth Wiseman

Her Brother's Keeper

"Wiseman has created a series in which the readers have a chance to peel back all the layers of the Amish secrets."

—*Romantic Times*, 4 1/2 stars and July 2015 Top Pick!

"Wiseman's new launch is edgier, taking on the tough issues of mental illness and suicide. Amish fiction fans seeking something a bit more thought-provoking and challenging than the usual fare will find this series debut a solid choice."

—*Library Journal*

The Promise

"The story of Mallory in *The Promise* uncovers the harsh reality American women can experience when they follow their hearts into a very different culture. Her story sheds light on how Islamic society is totally different from the Christian marriage covenant between one man and one woman. This novel is based on actual events, and Beth reached out to me during that time. It was heart-breaking to watch those real-life events unfolding. I salute the author's courage, persistence, and final triumph in writing a revealing and inspiring story."

—Nonie Darwish, author of *The Devil We Don't Know*, *Cruel and Usual Punishment*, and *Now They Call Me Infidel*

"*The Promise* is an only too realistic depiction of an American young woman motivated by the best humanitarian impulses and naïve trust facing instead betrayal, kidnapping, and life-threatening danger in Pakistan's lawless Pashtun tribal regions. But the story offers as well a reminder just as realistic that love and sacrifice are never wasted and that the hope of a loving heavenly Father is never absent in the most hopeless of situations."

—Jeanette Windle, author of *Veiled Freedom* (2010 ECPA Christian Book Award/Christy Award finalist), *Freedom's Stand* (2012 ECPA Christian Book Award/Carol Award finalist), and *Congo Dawn* (2013 Golden Scroll Novel of the Year)

The House that Love Built

"This sweet story with a hint of mystery is touching and emotional. Humor sprinkled throughout balances the occasional seriousness. The development of the love story is paced perfectly so that the reader gets a real sense of the characters."

—*Romantic Times*, 4-star review

"[*The House that Love Built*] is a warm, sweet tale of faith renewed and families restored."

—BookPage

Need You Now

"Wiseman, best known for her series of Amish novels, branches out into a wider world in this story of family, dependence, faith, and small-town Texas, offering a character for every reader to relate to . . . With an enjoyable cast of outside characters, *Need You Now* breaks the molds of small-town stereotypes. With issues ranging from special education and teen cutting to what makes a marriage strong, this is a compelling and worthy read."

—Booklist

"Wiseman gets to the heart of marriage and family interests in a way that will resonate with readers, with an intricately written plot featuring elements that seem to be ripped from current headlines. God provides hope for Wiseman's characters even in the most desperate situations."

—*Romantic Times*, 4-star review

"You may think you are familiar with Beth's wonderful story-telling gift but this is something new! This is a story that will stay with you for a long, long time. It's a story of hope when life seems hopeless. It's a story of how God can redeem the seemingly unredeemable. It's a message the Church, the world needs to hear."

—Sheila Walsh, author of *God Loves Broken People*

"Beth Wiseman tackles these difficult subjects with courage and grace. She reminds us that true healing can only come by being vulnerable and honest before our God who loves us more than anything."

—Deborah Bedford, bestselling author of *His Other Wife*, *A Rose by the Door*, and *The Penny* (coauthored with Joyce Meyer)

The Land of Canaan Novels

"Wiseman's voice is consistently compassionate and her words flow smoothly."

—*Publishers Weekly* review of *Seek Me with All Your Heart*

"Wiseman's third Land of Canaan novel overflows with romance, broken promises, a modern knight in shining armor, and hope at the end of the rainbow."

—*Romantic Times*

"In *Seek Me with All Your Heart*, Beth Wiseman offers readers a heartwarming story filled with complex characters and deep emotion. I instantly loved Emily, and eagerly turned each page, anxious to learn more about her past—and what future the Lord had in store for her."

—Shelley Shepard Gray, bestselling author of the Seasons of Sugarcreek series

"Wiseman has done it again! Beautifully compelling, *Seek Me with All Your Heart* is a heartwarming story of faith, family, and renewal. Her characters and descriptions are captivating, bringing the story to life with the turn of every page."

—Amy Clipston, bestselling author of *A Gift of Grace*

The Daughters of the Promise Novels

"Well-defined characters and story make for an enjoyable read."

—*Romantic Times* review of *Plain Pursuit*

"A touching, heartwarming story. Wiseman does a particularly great job of dealing with shunning, a controversial Amish practice that seems cruel and unnecessary to outsiders . . . If you're a fan of Amish fiction, don't miss *Plain Pursuit*!"

—Kathleen Fuller, author of The Middlefield Family novels

Love Bears All Things

Also by Beth Wiseman

The Amish Secrets Novels

Her Brother's Keeper

The Daughters of the Promise Novels

Plain Perfect

Plain Pursuit

Plain Promise

Plain Paradise

Plain Proposal

Plain Peace

The Land of Canaan Novels

Seek Me with All Your Heart

The Wonder of Your Love

His Love Endures Forever

Other Novels

Need You Now

The House that Love Built

The Promise

Novellas

A Choice to Forgive included in *An Amish Christmas*

A Change of Heart included in *An Amish Gathering*

Healing Hearts included in *An Amish Love*

A Perfect Plan included in *An Amish Wedding*

A Recipe for Hope included in *An Amish Kitchen*

Always Beautiful included in *An Amish Miracle*

Rooted in Love included in *An Amish Garden*

When Christmas Comes Again included in *An Amish Second Christmas*

In His Father's Arms included in *An Amish Cradle*

A Love for Irma Rose included in *An Amish Year*

Patchwork Perfect included in *An Amish Year*

A Cup Half Full included in *An Amish Home* (Available February 2017)

Love Bears All Things

An Amish Secrets novel

Beth Wiseman

Thomas Nelson
Since 1798

Published in Nashville, Tennessee, by Thomas Nelson. Thomas Nelson is a registered trademark of HarperCollins Christian Publishing, Inc.

Thomas Nelson titles may be purchased in bulk for educational, business, fund-raising, or sales promotional use. For information, please e-mail SpecialMarkets@ThomasNelson.com.

Scripture quotations are taken from the King James Version of the Bible.

Publisher's Note: This novel is a work of fiction. Names, characters, places, and incidents are either products of the author's imagination or used fictitiously. All characters are fictional, and any similarity to people living or dead is purely coincidental.

Library of Congress Cataloging-in-Publication Data

Names: Wiseman, Beth, 1962-author.
Title: Love bears all things / Beth Wiseman.
Description: Nashville: Thomas Nelson, [2016] | Series: Amish secrets; book 2
Identifiers: LCCN 2016001454 | ISBN 9780529118721 (softcover)
Subjects: LCSH: Amish—Fiction. | Family secrets—Fiction. | Man-woman relationships—Fiction. | GSAFD: Christian fiction. | Love stories.
Classification: LCC PS3623.I83 L69 2016 | DDC 813/.6—dc23 LC record available at http://lccn.loc.gov/2016001454

Printed in the United States of America

16 17 18 19 20 21 RRD 6 5 4 3 2 1

To Terry Newcomer

Pennsylvania Dutch Glossary

ab im kopp—off in the head; crazy
ach—oh
aenti—aunt
boppli—baby or babies
bruder—brother
daed—dad
danki—thank you
die Botschaft—an Amish newspaper; translated, it means "the Message"
Englisch—non-Amish
fraa—wife
gut—good
haus—house
kapp—prayer covering or cap
kinner—children
maedel—girl
mamm—mom

mei—my

mudder—mother

nee—no

onkel—uncle

Pennsylvania Deitsch—the language most commonly used by the Amish. Although commonly known as Pennsylvania Dutch, the language is actually a form of German (*Deutsch*).

rumschpringe—running-around period when a teenager turns sixteen years old

sohn—son

Wie bischt—How are you? or Hi there.

ya—yes

Charlotte leaned her head against the high-back chair in Dr. Levin's office. She closed her eyes, breathed in the familiar scent of lavender, and forced herself to relax the way Dr. Levin had taught her. She wondered why relaxation should take so much effort.

"Tell me again about this vision you keep having." Maureen Levin was good at peeling back the layers of Charlotte's psyche, and most of the counseling sessions had been helpful. But one thing continued to niggle at Charlotte. She slowly exhaled, then opened her eyes.

"I've told you everything I can remember. And it's not really a vision. More like a secret. A secret that I'm hiding from myself." She shrugged. "Maybe I dreamed it and just can't shake the images."

"Do you think you dreamed it?" Dr. Levin took off

a pair of red reading glasses and rested her hands on a stack of files.

"No. But every time I try to focus on it, I get a headache and my chest hurts."

Dr. Levin gazed across her desk at Charlotte. "Do you think the child in the vision is a younger version of yourself?"

Charlotte had already put herself through a vigorous round of diagnostics without success. "Maybe."

"What do you think younger Charlotte may be trying to tell you?"

Sighing, Charlotte searched her mind, trying to bring forth something that might help her understand why a midnight trip to the store for ice cream had left her with such an unsettled, anxious feeling the past few weeks. She'd already told Dr. Levin all this, but she suspected her therapist was hoping she'd recall something else by retelling it. "I was still upset about the breakup with Ryan, and I couldn't sleep, so I went to get some ice cream." She paused as the weight of the vision, memory—whatever it was—settled into her chest, sending waves of thunder to her temples. "I saw the little girl and the woman."

"And you said the woman resembled your mother?"

Charlotte nodded. "Yeah. Maybe. From what I remember of her." She cringed, wanting to stop but knowing Dr. Levin would keep pushing. "I just don't know if remembering is good. Maybe I should work at forgetting instead."

Dr. Levin put her glasses back on and stared down at a yellow pad in her lap. "You told me a couple of weeks ago that this woman and child at the store reminded you of something, but that you didn't know what. You also said that the woman was wearing a dark green dress and the little girl was wearing a purple dress, correct?"

Charlotte took another deep breath. "I hate the color purple." Her bottom lip trembled as a chill ran up her spine.

Dr. Levin lifted her eyes to Charlotte's. "This is the first time you've mentioned this, that you dislike the color purple. Perhaps you associate that color with something unpleasant that happened when you were young, and seeing those people triggered a memory."

"I think I would like to stuff that memory back where it came from if it's going to cause me this much aggravation."

"What upsets you more, the recollection itself or the frustration that you can't remember the details?"

Charlotte wanted to curse Ryan for setting up these sessions with his aunt, but she had to admit she liked Dr. Levin. A lot more than she liked Ryan these days. "Both," she finally said. "It scares me that something I don't even remember has this kind of effect on me."

"Charlotte, you've been through a lot. Your brother's suicide, the breakup with Ryan, and . . . didn't you say money was an issue right now?"

Charlotte felt her cheeks flush, wishing she hadn't mentioned her finances during a prior visit. "I lost some clients, and several are behind in paying me. But I feel like it will get better soon."

"I know that your situation with Ryan has changed, but he offered to keep paying for you to come see me weekly." Dr. Levin was writing on the pad in her lap. Charlotte wondered what level of crazy Dr. Levin had assigned her. "And I hope you know, his being my nephew has no bearing on anything," she added without looking up.

"I know." Charlotte believed her, but she didn't want Ryan's charity. She'd already decided that this would be her last session, but she nodded anyway. Dr. Levin had served her purpose. She'd helped Charlotte work through some straggling issues about her childhood and her brother's death. This recent and unexpected recollection had come out of nowhere, and Charlotte hoped it would scurry back to where it came from soon. "I remember something else." Charlotte's voice hitched in her throat as she recalled another detail. "They—the lady and the girl—were barefoot."

Dr. Levin continued to write for a few moments before she looked up at Charlotte. "Okay. To summarize, you've said that you ran into a woman and child while on a random trip to the convenience store for ice cream. The woman looked like your mother, from what you can recall, and she was wearing a dark green dress. The little girl had on a purple dress with white trim. And they weren't wearing any shoes." Dr. Levin glanced at her pad.

"And this scene was somehow familiar to you and has left you feeling unsettled since then."

"We've been through all this," Charlotte said softly. "Maybe it means nothing. It's just a vague memory or something that isn't pertinent to my life."

Dr. Levin stared long and hard at Charlotte, even though her eyes shone with a kindness Charlotte had noticed on her first visit. "Do you believe that?"

Not for a minute. She thought about the promise she'd made to herself—and God—awhile back. That she would never tell another lie. But as much as she'd meant to keep that promise, she looked directly at Dr. Levin and said, "Yes, I do." Maybe if she convinced herself that the memory was unimportant, that would trump a potential lie.

Dr. Levin locked eyes with Charlotte, and in that moment, she could see the resemblance between her and Ryan. Those seemingly transparent, grayish-blue eyes that blazed the distance between two people, searching, wondering, trying to understand Charlotte.

"You told me you spent time with the Amish people in Pennsylvania not too long ago." Dr. Levin lightly tapped her pen against the pad of paper. "Don't the Amish people go barefoot a lot? Have you associated this recollection with your time in Pennsylvania in any way?"

Charlotte let the thought swim around for a few moments. "No."

Not until now.

~

Following a Sonic drive-through lunch, Charlotte couldn't shrug the feeling that maybe her session with Dr. Levin had peeled back another layer. She'd blocked out so many things about her parents and her time in foster care. In her effort to be normal, maybe she'd dreamed up this woman and child in Amish clothes as a way of self-comfort—a way to live the peaceful life she'd never had, where a loving mother and daughter stepped out for ice cream. *But at midnight?*

She slurped the last of her chocolate shake as she walked the long corridor to her apartment, slowing her steps when she noticed an envelope taped to the door. It was the third one this month. The first two were warnings that her rent was past due, which she was acutely aware of. She stuffed it in her purse and hurried back to her mailbox downstairs, disappointed that the only thing inside was an electric bill. On her way back up to her apartment, she called the client she'd done the big editing project for—the lady who owed Charlotte the most. No answer—again.

She'd barely opened her front door when Buddy made his way across the living room and squatted on all fours next to her. "Hi, baby." She scratched the Chihuahua's ears as she slipped out of her flip-flops, tossing her purse on the couch. Then she padded across the carpet to her bedroom, returning with a shoe box tucked under one arm. She set it right inside the entryway and stared at it on the floor.

After a few moments, she held her left hand at arm's length and admired the two-carat tennis bracelet Ryan had given her. It would be the last time she'd see the gorgeous piece of jewelry. A token of his love for her, he'd said.

Recoiling her hand, she unhooked the latch and put the bracelet in the shiny white container it had come in, then placed it into the box with Ryan's other things—a striped tie and three dollars in change he'd left on her kitchen counter.

I will not cry. I will not cry. I will not cry.

Buddy laid his head on one of Charlotte's bare feet. Her sweet pup's droopy eyes stared up at her as his tongue swept gently across her toes. Even her faithful companion was sad.

Her cell phone rang three times before she scooped Buddy into her arms and forced herself to walk across the living room. Maybe Ryan was calling to say he wasn't coming over after all. Charlotte took her cell phone out of her purse, but when she saw the caller ID, she just stared at the number. *Hannah.*

As much as she loved Hannah and her family, just hearing her Amish friend's voice would bring a river of tears, and now was not the time for crying. She wanted Ryan to see that her life would go on just fine without him.

Which, of course, it won't. Charlotte didn't think her eyes had been dry for more than an hour over the past week.

She eyed her phone and watched it vibrate with a new voice mail. Hannah rarely called. Cell phones in Amish families were mostly for emergencies—at least that's the way it was supposed to be. She put a hand to her chest and sucked in a big gulp of air when there was a knock at the door. *God, give me strength.* She'd been praying, but the Lord must have deemed her unworthy of a life with Ryan.

Charlotte set Buddy on the couch and shuffled across the living room, stopping short of the front door. She released her breath, picked up the small box, and reached for the doorknob.

As she stared at the man she'd hoped to marry someday, she fought the urge to rush into his arms and beg for forgiveness. Again. But somewhere deep in her soul, she knew it was over between them. Everything that could be said had been said, and there was no recovering what they'd once had. But it was a reality she didn't want to face, so she clung to the tiniest bit of hope in an effort to stay sane.

Ryan looked past Charlotte when Buddy scurried across the floor toward them. "Hey, Buddy." He picked up the dog as a smile lit his face. It wasn't so long ago that Ryan greeted her with the same enthusiasm. He nuzzled Buddy for a few moments before he set him down, then he found Charlotte's gaze and held it for a long while before he said, "Did you find a letter from the landlord taped to your door?"

"Um . . ." She turned toward the couch where her purse was. "Yeah, just a few minutes ago, but I haven't opened it yet. I know I'm late on my rent. I've already gotten two notices, but I'm waiting on a check."

Ryan held his position just inside the front door as he sighed. "You've been evicted, Charlotte."

"What?" she answered in a squeaky voice, her heart rate soaring.

"What did you think would happen if you didn't pay your rent or communicate with the apartment manager?" He spoke in a tone that made Charlotte feel like a child. "They've tried to call you and also serve you with papers twice, and that's all that's required by law. And since I'm listed as your emergency contact, they were knocking at my door this afternoon. I just happened to be working from home today."

"They probably called the number for my landline, the one I gave them when I moved in. But I don't have it anymore. I just have my cell phone." She lowered her eyes as a knot built in her throat. "I thought I had more time, and—"

"Charlotte, I want only good things for you, but you need to figure out a way to get off this financial hamster wheel you've been riding." He took a deep breath and let it out slowly. "As much as I'd like to help you, I can't this time."

"I'll be okay. Really." She blinked back tears and lifted her chin as she tried to maintain a tiny bit of pride. "When my checks finally arrive, I'll be fine." She picked up the box with Ryan's things and held it out, trying hard to smile, but trying even harder not to cry.

"I told you I don't really need that stuff." He scooped Buddy into his arms again and scratched behind the dog's ears, not even looking at Charlotte, as if shattering her life had no lasting effect on him.

Charlotte shrugged. "Well, what am I going to do with a tie?" She pushed the box at him until he finally put Buddy down and took it. "The bracelet's in there too."

"Charlotte . . ." Ryan sighed and finally looked her in the eye. "It doesn't have to be this way. We were friends for a long time before this. I still want you in my life."

"Are you kidding me?" She regretted the outburst right away. Her plan had been not to react, no matter what, to remain detached. But tears gathered in the corners of her eyes, and as she attempted to blink them away, she added, "I don't want to be your *friend*."

Ryan lifted the lid from the box, pulled out the small white jewelry box, and eyed the bracelet. "I told you to keep this. If you don't want to wear it, you should sell it."

Charlotte bit her bottom lip and shook her head, even though she suspected the bracelet would bring in enough money to catch her up on rent. It didn't feel right.

Ryan sighed again as he snapped the white box closed and put everything back as it was, tucking the shoe box under his arm. He eyed the dog at his feet, and Charlotte wondered who Ryan was going to miss the most—her or Buddy. Ryan probably deserved joint custody of Buddy. They'd picked him out at the shelter together, and Ryan loved the dog as much as Charlotte did. Ryan had paid for all of Buddy's shots and medications at the vet's office. She wished he didn't know her financial situation. It just added another layer of humiliation.

"Anyway, it doesn't have to be like this," he repeated, ignoring her comment about not wanting to be just friends.

"How should it be, Ryan?" She bit her bottom lip again as she recalled the scene in his living room two weeks ago, her screaming as he tried to defend himself. Charlotte knew she'd gone too far when she heaved a candy bowl at the fireplace, shattering it to pieces while Hershey's Kisses rolled across the floor amid shards of glass.

"I don't know how it should be, honestly. I just know that I want you in my life in some capacity." He said the words as if he were giving a presentation for work.

"Just go," she said as a tear slipped down her cheek. *Plan foiled.* This was not how she wanted to present herself, as the pitiful girl who got dumped, whose heart was broken. But that's exactly who she was, and she was starting to think that was who she'd always be. The girl with a broken heart who was abused as a child, whose brother had killed himself, whose parents were MIA—and now the one man she'd pinned all her hopes and dreams on had kicked her to the curb.

He turned to leave but hadn't gotten far when Charlotte said, "Ryan?" He slowly turned around.

Don't do it. Stay quiet. Maintain a little dignity.

"Is there any . . . any way that . . ." The dam broke, and tears poured down her face. ". . . that maybe we could try . . . to . . ." She held her breath, feeling a sliver of optimism when Ryan's eyes filled with tears too. That should have made her happy, to see him hurting. But it didn't.

He shook his head, and without saying anything, he turned and walked away.

Charlotte closed the door and stared at it, the scent of Ryan's cologne lingering. After a few moments, she shuffled back across the living room and threw herself onto the couch so she could continue her meltdown. But her eyes went back to the door, where Buddy was still standing, staring the same way Charlotte had.

"He's not coming back, Buddy," she said softly as she straightened her dog's favorite blue blanket, patting it until she finally got his attention. With his head hung and his tail between his legs, Buddy made his way to her. Even though she and Ryan hadn't lived together, he'd been at her apartment a lot. As she stroked Buddy's back, she wondered how much an animal felt such a loss. "It's my fault, not yours," she said as she continued to love on him. *Apparently, I have trust issues.*

After a few minutes, she dragged herself off the couch, picked up her cell phone from the kitchen bar, and pushed the voice mail button. When she heard Hannah's voice, more tears came. She hadn't told her friend about the breakup yet, and she longed for the comfort her Amish family would offer her. Maybe her self-analysis about the woman and little girl had been correct after all.

But when Charlotte heard Hannah sniffle, she stifled her own cries to listen to the message. "Jacob left. He left us. He doesn't want to be Amish." *What?* There was a long pause. "*Mamm* is frantic. We found a note two days ago, but we thought he'd be back. We haven't heard anything and now we're really worried. Why would he do this? He and Annie were supposed to get married in the fall." Hannah sniffled again. "Please call me when you can."

Charlotte hit redial on the phone and walked to the couch to sit by Buddy, wondering why life had a way of throwing curveballs that plunked you in the face when you least expected it.

"Hannah, it's me. I got your message. What in the world do you think made Jacob leave?" Charlotte slouched into the white cushions next to Buddy. "Were he and Annie fighting?"

"*Nee.* Annie says they weren't squabbling or anything." Hannah exhaled. "*Mamm* went to Annie's house this morning and showed her the letter. Jacob didn't really give a reason, just that he couldn't stay in Lancaster County. He asked everyone to forgive his choice, and he said to tell Annie that he loves her—and us—very much. But he didn't even say where he was going."

"I can't believe he left." Charlotte wasn't as surprised as she let on, recalling her time in Lancaster County at the end of last year. Jacob had always been much more worldly than the others. He loved anything to do with space and the universe, and he even owned a telescope. He'd always been preoccupied with things happening outside of their community. And if Charlotte's experiences were any example, men were generally fickle, unsure of what they wanted. But she knew enough about the Amish to know that leaving the community was rare. Most kids stayed, even after having a chance to explore the outside world through their *rumschpringe*, beginning at age sixteen. Jacob wasn't even eighteen yet.

"I bet he'll come back," Charlotte offered, trying to stay afloat amid her own troubles. She lay back on the couch next to Buddy, crossed one ankle over the other, and settled her head against the armrest of the couch. Occasionally she glanced toward the front door, willing Ryan to return, to say he'd made a horrible mistake, that he loved her no matter what.

"I don't know, Charlotte. Jacob has always been . . . different. *Mamm* has always worried this might happen someday. She actually cried joyful tears when she found out Jacob wanted to marry Annie. She took that as a sure sign that Jacob wouldn't leave. But *Mamm* and *Daed* are so upset now that he's gone. We all are. But we have to believe that Jacob will think about what he's doing and choose to come back. We hope he will make that choice sooner instead of later, but he will always be welcome home."

Home. Charlotte wondered where her home was going to be. She probably only had until the end of the month to be out of her apartment. Her mind was swirling, and she was having trouble staying focused on the conversation, but she wanted to be reassuring to her friend.

"Maybe Jacob just needs some time away from everyone to think about things." Charlotte wasn't sure Jacob had ever been out of Lancaster County. "Then he'll be back."

Hannah's family would forgive Jacob for most anything. That was the Amish way. Charlotte recalled all the lies she'd told Hannah and her family a few months ago, all in an attempt to find out why her only brother had committed suicide in their Amish community. Hannah, Jacob, and their mother Lena had forgiven Charlotte, but she wasn't sure about Hannah's father. Amos was a quiet man, but Charlotte could still recall the anger etched across the older man's face when he'd learned the truth.

Following her cancer diagnosis, Lena had needed chemo at MD Anderson, and she'd stayed with Charlotte in Houston. They'd formed a bond that Charlotte had never known with her own mother, and Amos always sent his regards to Charlotte. But Charlotte wasn't sure if she'd ever be completely back in Amos's good graces.

Looking back, she was still surprised that it took Hannah and her family as long as it did to figure out that Charlotte wasn't really their cousin from Beeville, that she wasn't even Amish. But Charlotte would have eventually told them. The lies had been suffocating her. She had a lot of memories from her time in Lancaster County—good and bad. But it was the good ones she held tightly to, recalling them when she needed to feel loved. Like now. She sniffled and quietly blew her nose.

"What's wrong, Charlotte? You sound like you're crying." Hannah said it with such tenderness that moisture pooled in Charlotte's eyes. She squeezed her eyes closed and allowed the tears to spill down her cheeks.

"You have enough to worry about with Jacob and—" Her voice cracked before she could finish.

"Tell me. What is it?" Hannah's sweet voice only made Charlotte cry harder.

"Ryan broke up with me."

There was a long silence before Hannah responded. "I'm so sorry. What happened?"

Charlotte wiped her eyes and sat up, moving to sit Indian style. "It's a long story, but I thought Ryan was cheating on me with a woman named Shelley, someone he works with. I became so obsessed about it that I, uh . . . checked his text messages." She squeezed her eyes closed again for a few moments. "He caught me, and things just sort of blew up." Sniffling, she decided not to mention the candy bowl. "As it turns out, he wasn't involved with her in a romantic way. I'm ashamed that I stooped to that level, to check his messages. And now I'm just sad."

Sad was an understatement. She thought about Ethan and wondered how low he must have felt to think that suicide was his only option. Charlotte was a survivor and would never do anything to hurt herself, but she wondered why God had shown her how true love could feel, only to take it away from her.

"I can hear how much you're hurting, Charlotte. But you mustn't feel shame. We all do things we regret, but God forgives us, and to hold on to shame doesn't honor God. We love you and will be praying for your heart to heal."

Hannah always helped Charlotte to see things from a spiritual perspective, even at a time when her own family was in crisis. "Thank you. I love all of you too." She reached for the box of tissues as Buddy snored on the couch next to her. She dabbed at her eyes, wondering how she was going to get enough money for a deposit on another apartment. She didn't have any blood relatives to turn to. She'd gotten detached from most of her girlfriends since she'd been spending so much time with Ryan. And even though sadness had taken hold of her, fear of being homeless was starting to take a front seat. No one but Ryan and Dr. Levin knew about her financial troubles. She was going to be truthful with Hannah, but she wasn't up to sharing the entire truth right now.

She squeezed her eyes closed and grimaced. "I'm having a little trouble with some of my clients paying me. I'm going to move at the end of the month, hopefully somewhere a little cheaper." She took a deep breath and blew it out slowly. "And it's my fault too. I've lost my focus on work during this whole breakup with Ryan."

Hannah waited to respond, then said, "You should move here."

"Huh?"

"You've said that the nature of your job will let you work from anywhere, and you own a house free and clear right here in Lancaster County."

The house. Ethan's house that he'd left to her. "Yeah, I own a house that doesn't have electricity."

Hannah chuckled. "*Ya*, well . . . it's not so bad. You managed while you were staying with us before. But you could always have electricity installed."

That takes money. "And I don't know if I could live there, Hannah. I mean, because that's where Ethan lived, and—"

"I understand."

"But if I could get it sold, that would certainly help my financial situation. Didn't you say that Isaac was done with all the repairs and painting?" Charlotte had barely squeaked out the money for that, and she suspected Hannah's fiancé hadn't charged her for his time, just the supplies. "If so, I should probably get it listed to sell."

"*Ya*. He's done." Hannah huffed. "It would sure be fun if you lived nearby."

Charlotte let the thought wander around in her head, but it wasn't long before the woman and little girl flashed in her mind again. She wondered if her brother had felt drawn to Amish country because of some distant memory. She wished she could ask him. But if anyone might know, it would be Hannah, since her friend had been engaged to her brother before he died.

"Hannah, I'm so sorry to be dumping my problems on you while all this is going on with Jacob, but I need to ask you something, then I'll let you go."

"*Ya*, okay. What is it?"

Charlotte took a deep breath. "I know Ethan talked to you about our childhood and the couple of years we both spent in foster care, but did he ever mention anything . . ." Charlotte paused. She wasn't even sure how to explain this odd recollection she seemed to be having.

"Did he mention what?"

Charlotte did her best to explain to Hannah, then shrugged. "If the woman and the little girl were dressed like the Amish, it seems odd that I'd see myself as the child and my mother as the adult. My counselor suggested that, but I don't know. And if I was going to have some weird memory pop up like that, you'd think it would have happened last time I was in Amish country." She shook her head. "I'm just going to try not to think about it. I have enough on my plate."

"Did the woman or child have on a *kapp*?"

Charlotte's heart pounded as her head started to hurt. Dr. Levin hadn't thought to ask that question. She brought a hand to her chest. "The woman and little girl at the convenience store didn't have on any type of prayer covering." Her heart seemed to skip a beat as a memory flashed from somewhere deep in her mind. "But when I see a woman and child in my head, the woman in the green dress *does* have a *kapp* on. What does that mean?" Her voice was louder than normal as she tried to remember more.

"I don't know. But if you can't move here, maybe a visit here will help you recall whatever it is that's bothering you."

"Hannah, I'd love nothing more than to come for a visit, but now probably isn't the best time, with Jacob having left. And I need to save all of my money to get moved." *Assuming any comes in the mail.* Charlotte dug in her purse for the envelope that had been taped to her door. She ripped it open, scanned through some legal stuff, and landed on the part where she had to be out by the end of the month. In two and a half weeks.

She lifted herself off the couch and walked to the mirror in the entryway of her apartment—dark circles under swollen eyes, flushed cheeks from crying, and hair that hadn't seen a brush in a while. "Why is it that I keep trying to live a good life, and God keeps challenging me at every turn?"

"Sweet Charlotte. I know it's hard to understand God's will, and even harder to accept it sometimes. After Ethan died, I was sure I would never be happy again. But I am happy with Isaac, very happy. And you will find happiness too. I'm sorry about you and Ryan, and I'm sorry you feel like you must move. But I'm also feeling selfish, too, about the possibility that maybe you could live here."

"I'll think about it." In truth, Charlotte wasn't ready to be that far away from Ryan, just in case he changed his mind. "Right now, I just hope you hear from Jacob."

"*Ya*, I hope so. Annie is beside herself distraught. She cried the whole time *Mamm* was at her house. *Daed* isn't saying much, but you know how quiet he is most of the time."

Charlotte agreed. Again, she wondered if Hannah's father had truly forgiven her.

After they'd ended the conversation, Charlotte took a long, hot bath, then snuggled into her covers. Sleep was her only relief since there was no cure for a broken heart. Logically, she knew that time would heal her hurt. But at the moment, the pain seemed unbearable, so she tried to focus on Jacob, pondering how he could leave Annie and his family. Across the miles, Charlotte's heart hurt for Annie, a young woman Charlotte had met only a couple of times during her stay in Lancaster County.

But her thoughts drifted away from Ryan, Jacob, Annie, and her financial issues, replaced by thoughts of the woman and child. She was almost asleep when she bolted up in bed and grabbed her chest. Gasping, she took deep breaths to calm herself as she recalled something else.

She'd heard squealing tires.

Two

Jacob huddled on a bench outside the train station, wishing he'd brought a heavier coat, like the one he kept on a hook by the front door. He'd left in such a hurry, he hadn't realized how chilly it was until he'd settled into the backseat of the cab. Flurries of snow had dotted the windshield on the way to the station, which was unusual for March. But Jacob was pretty sure it would be warmer where he was going. It had been a slow ride to the station, with plenty of time for him to think about what he was doing. What kind of man would leave the woman he loved to start a new life—a life in the *Englisch* world? But it was all Jacob had thought about for months. He'd tried to will away the idea, convinced that all this prodding to leave was the work of the devil. He'd even stayed in town at a cheap motel overnight, hoping he'd wake up with a notion to stay in Lancaster County. But here he was at the train station, still looking to leave.

He blew air into his cupped hands and felt downright dumb that he'd forgotten his gloves too. Glancing at his small suitcase, he wondered what else he'd left behind.

Jacob boarded the train when it was time, and as he stared out the window, he swallowed back the knot in his throat and wondered again if he could live without Annie. But he couldn't stay in Paradise, Pennsylvania, even if it was a place filled with love, family, hard work, and strong faith—ideals he'd always cherished. His desire to live in the outside world had crushed his spirit about everything else. Even sharing a life with the girl he loved.

As the train wheels rumbled against the track, the whistle blew and the train picked up speed. Jacob settled into his seat and tried to relax. But the faster the train went, the faster his heart thumped, and by the time they'd cleared the station and reached full speed, Jacob feared his heart might give out. His chest tightened to the point that he couldn't breathe. Normally he would pray. But God was surely disappointed in him, and it didn't seem right to seek help from the Lord while fleeing from home. He probably deserved the suffering, so he pulled his eyes from the window, leaned back against the seat, and tried to steady his breathing.

Charlotte glanced around her living room at all the boxes she'd managed to pack in the past day and a half. She'd filled out an application for an apartment online and managed to finish an editing job early that morning. *Now, if only a check would arrive.*

She picked up an old fax machine and carried it to the to-be-pawned pile, where it joined an outdated inkjet printer, a digital camera, an old iPhone, and a box of costume jewelry that she didn't wear anymore. She'd only done business with a pawnshop once in her life. Her parents had left her and Ethan alone for two days. Neither of them was even ten years old at the time. Ethan had a watch he'd gotten as a gift during one of their better Christmases, and they'd pawned it for five dollars to get some food.

Ryan's words kept coming at her like daggers: *You need to figure out a way to get off this financial hamster wheel you've been riding.* Maybe once Ryan saw that Charlotte was getting her finances in order, he'd change his mind and give them a second chance. And she'd spent time with Dr. Levin learning ways to be more trusting.

Blinking back tears, she knew this wasn't a time to fall apart. She needed to check with the kid who lived two apartments down. He did odd jobs for some of her neighbors sometimes. Maybe he and a couple of friends could move her things more cheaply than a moving company. She needed to schedule her electricity to be turned off and arrange to have her mail forwarded.

Please let the application for this new apartment get approved. And please, dear God, let there be a check in the mail soon.

"We're gonna be okay," she said to Buddy as she sat down beside him on the couch and scratched him behind the ears. When her cell phone rang, she hurried to the kitchen counter where she'd left it, hoping—like always—that it was Ryan. Or maybe it was Hannah saying they'd heard from Jacob.

Pam Rutherford. Frowning, she answered it. Charlotte had recently bumped into her high school friend at the post office. They hadn't seen each other in years and promised to get together. Charlotte had canceled twice, both times due to work projects.

"I am not letting you cancel on me this time," Pam said after Charlotte answered. "My husband is starting to think we were never best friends in school." She laughed, and right away Charlotte smiled, glad that Pam still seemed like the fun person she was in school.

"I am absolutely not canceling." Charlotte could probably list a dozen reasons why she should, but maybe a night out was exactly what she needed. It would be fun to catch up, and Pam was eager for Charlotte to meet her husband. Plus, it was a free meal, and Charlotte hadn't been to Carrabba's Italian Grill since the last time she'd been there with Ryan.

"Don't forget to wear green!"

St. Patrick's Day. Maybe all the festivity of the evening

would keep her mind off her problems long enough to remember what it was like to have a good time.

After they confirmed the time, Charlotte glanced at Buddy snoozing on the couch, oblivious to the big move they were about to make. But her pup bolted upright when there was a knock at the door, jumping from the couch and scurrying alongside Charlotte. She looked through the peephole, threw her hand over her mouth, and pulled the door open.

~

Jacob took off his straw hat and let out a heavy sigh. "*Wie bischt*, Charlotte."

His *Englisch* friend finally closed her mouth and stepped aside so he could enter her apartment, closing the door behind him. Jacob's jacket was folded over his arm as he carried the old brown suitcase across the threshold, sidestepping a little dog that was barking. The boxy piece of luggage with two gold-plated locks surely wasn't fit for big-city life, but it was all he could find at the time. He set the suitcase down and reached into his pocket for a handkerchief, then dabbed at the sweat beading on his forehead. He knew it would be warmer in Texas than Pennsylvania in March, but he didn't think it would be like this.

"What are you doing here?" Charlotte put her hands on her hips, stared at him for a few moments, then put her arms around his neck and squeezed. As she eased away from him, he studied her face—her swollen, red eyes. The dog was growling and showing his teeth, but Charlotte didn't seem to notice.

"Why have you been crying?"

She took his jacket from him, tossed it on the couch, then turned to face him again, her hands back on her hips. Jacob stood perfectly still, unsure if the animal at his feet was going to bite him. The little fellow seemed to pack a lot of energy for being so small.

"Let's don't worry about me right now. Hannah called—your family is frantic. And how could you leave Annie like this?" She took a quick breath, then pointed a finger at him. "You need to call them. Right now."

Jacob's feet were rooted to the floor, still in the entryway, mostly due to the dog. But he lowered his head, knowing he hadn't done right by his family or Annie. After a few seconds, he looked back at her. "I couldn't stay, Charlotte. I just couldn't. There's a whole world out here . . ." He waved his arm around her apartment, the feel of the cool air a reminder of what he'd left behind. "I thirst for knowledge."

Charlotte took a few steps toward him as she cocked her head to one side. "Thirst for knowledge?" She raised an eyebrow, then she finally picked up her dog and he stopped barking.

"I read that in a book." He glanced around her apartment again, at her white couch, two wicker chairs, glass coffee table, and lots of boxes everywhere. He'd dreamed about living in a fancy place like this, burying his head in books, watching television, and learning new things. He took his hat off, glanced around for a hook by the door, then set it on top of his suitcase, frowning. "Are you moving?"

Charlotte nodded. "Yes, and I'll explain about that later. We have to call your family. But first, are you hungry? How did you get here?"

Jacob shook his head. "*Nee.* I'm thirsty, though. And I could use a shower. It took a long time to get here by train."

Charlotte pointed to the couch. "Sit. I'll go get us some iced tea, then we'll figure this out." Thankfully, she carried the dog with her.

Jacob slowly eased onto her white couch, the cushions soft and welcoming. He noticed a tissue box on the end table along with a whole mess of wadded-up tissues.

"What's wrong, Charlotte?" he asked when she walked back into the living room carrying two glasses. "Why have you been crying? And why are you moving?"

She sat down beside him, gave him a glass of tea, and put hers on the coffee table. Her little dog growled once but then jumped up on Charlotte's lap.

"Ryan and I broke up, and it's still fresh, so I cry sometimes. And yes, I'm moving soon. But right now, I want to talk about you." Taking a deep breath, she closed her eyes for a few seconds before she looked back at him. "So, is this temporary, just a vacation or something?"

Jacob shrugged. "I don't know." That was the truth. "I just felt like a corralled animal without enough pasture to roam."

Charlotte tucked her long brown hair behind her ears as she repositioned her dog and twisted to face him. "Is this about Annie? Do you feel like she isn't the one? If she's not, that's okay. But you don't have to leave your whole life behind. Or is it your whole life that feels stifled?"

Jacob frowned, unsure what *stifled* meant. He was educated more than most people in his community, having schooled himself through books long past the eighth grade, but he'd have to look up *stifled* later. "I just couldn't stay there anymore. I love Annie. I really do, but . . ." He glanced around Charlotte's apartment again, then locked eyes with her. "I was going to see if I can stay with you for a while." His eyes darted from one box to another. "But, uh . . . how long will you be here?"

Charlotte sighed. "Not long, just until the end of the month." She walked around the corner and returned with her mobile phone. She thrust her arm out as she stood in front of him. "But right now, you need to call Hannah or your parents to let them know where you are. They are worried sick."

"I left a note." He cringed. It was a cowardly way to handle things, and he still wasn't feeling very brave. "Can you call them?"

"Jacob, really? Don't you think you should be the one to do that?"

He blinked his eyes a few times and felt his cheeks turning red. *What kind of man shirks his responsibilities like this?* He opened his mouth to speak, but nothing came out.

"Fine," she said. "I'll call them. I'll tell them you are going to stay here for now. They'll be relieved to know you're okay. But then you need to go home."

"*Nee*. I just got here. I don't want to go back." He stood up and looped his thumbs beneath his suspenders. "I ain't going back," he repeated under his breath as he hung his head.

Charlotte made a weird growling sound. "Jacob, this is not a good time for this. I have to be out of this apartment by the end of the month." She raised her shoulders, then let them drop slowly.

"But you'll have a new apartment, *ya*?"

Charlotte nodded. "Hopefully. I mean, yes . . . I'll have another place to live." She pulled her eyes from his as she rubbed her forehead and made that weird sound again. "*Grr* . . . I can't believe you left home like this without telling anyone where you were going."

Jacob reached into the pocket of his trousers and pulled out a wad of cash. "I've got lots of money, if that's what you're worried about. I have almost a thousand dollars." Jacob stood taller. "I'm not going back. I'll go to a local hostel or breakfast inn."

Charlotte rolled her eyes as her hands flew to her hips again. "Jacob, you are in the big city of Houston, and in the Galleria area. You are not going to find hostels, and any bed-and-breakfasts will most likely be upscale and out of your price range. You can stay in a hotel, but even a cheap one is going to run you at least a hundred dollars per night. Is that really how you want to spend your money?" She drew in a breath. "And besides, it's not that I don't want you here. I just think you are too far from home to be seventeen years old and trying to make adult decisions. I'm calling Hannah right now to let her know you're safe. You can stay for a few days." She smiled. "You can help me pack."

Finally, a break. "*Ya*, I can do that. And you can help me find a place to live."

Charlotte stomped her foot and started to say something, but instead she brought her phone closer to her cheek. "Well, you're not going to believe this, but Jacob is safe. He's here, at my apartment." She nodded. "Yes, yes. He's fine. I think he just needs a few days to think things through, then I'll put him on a train back home."

"I'm not going back." He spoke louder than the last few times he'd told her, but she ignored him and finally hung up with Hannah.

Charlotte fell onto her couch next to her dog, sighing. "Jacob, Houston is nothing like where you live. It's busy and fast . . . and—"

Jacob sat down beside her. "Kinda smelly too." He

grinned. And finally Charlotte did too. He was sure he'd made the right choice to come here.

~

Charlotte considered canceling on Pam again, but a third time might put the reestablished friendship at risk, and without Ryan in the picture, Charlotte could use a friend now. It felt good to slip on a pretty green dress she'd only worn once. She took some extra time curling her hair and sprayed on a perfume she saved for special occasions.

"Are you sure you'll be okay while I'm gone?" she asked Jacob as she grabbed her purse.

Her house guest had obviously mastered the remote control for the television while Charlotte had showered and gotten ready. He was busily flipping through the channels. "*Ya*. I'll be fine."

"I'm afraid there isn't a ton of food here, but there are some frozen dinners you can heat in the microwave, and there's sandwich stuff." She paused, recalling how much Jacob could eat, even though his lanky build wasn't reflective of such a healthy appetite. "You're sure you don't want to go?"

"*Nee.* You said you haven't seen your friend in a while, and it sounds like a fancy place." Jacob frowned. He'd removed his suspenders and untucked his shirt, but with his cropped blond bangs, he still screamed Amish. Charlotte had never seen an Amish person in Houston.

He might have had to endure some stares, but she would have happily taken him along. She felt sure Pam would have been fine with it. “Well, okay. I’ll probably be back in a couple of hours. I’ll lock the door behind me.”

Charlotte found Pam and her husband waiting right inside the restaurant entrance, and after Pam introduced Charlotte to her husband—Phillip—they were escorted to a table. All the while, Charlotte breathed in the aroma of Italian spices and bread baking. In the distance she could see meat grilling on open flames in the kitchen area.

She passed on the house wine and opted for a glass of Kendall-Jackson chardonnay, following Pam’s lead. She wasn’t much of a drinker, but the evening seemed to call for a glass of vino to go with the fabulous dinner she was about to have. She glanced around at all the couples, green attire dominating the evening, mostly on the women. But there were a few guys sporting green shirts in celebration of St. Patrick’s Day.

A few moments later, she thanked the waiter for her wine and started looking over the menu. The only thing that would have made the evening perfect was Ryan sitting next to her.

She ordered the chicken parmesan with fettuccine and a Caesar salad, and then told Pam and Phillip about her unexpected visitor.

“You definitely could have brought your young Amish friend tonight,” Pam said, smiling. “I don’t know anything about the Amish. I would have enjoyed chatting with him."

"I would have called to check with y'all first, but he was tired, and they don't watch TV in Amish country, so he was joyfully flipping through the channels when I left." Charlotte smiled, happy she had come.

"It's so great to see you," Pam said as she studied Charlotte for a few moments. "And, wow, you look amazing."

Charlotte had worked extra hard to cover the dark circles underneath her eyes. Pam was an attractive woman, tall and slender with soft blond curls that rested just above her shoulders, and blue eyes that Charlotte knew were enhanced by colored contacts. "So do you," Charlotte said, smiling. She looked over at Phillip. "So how did you two meet?"

Phillip finished a bite of bread, dabbed his mouth with a napkin, and glanced at his wife. "We met in college, and even though college romances don't always work out, ours did. We got married two months after we graduated."

Charlotte quickly calculated that Pam and Phillip had been married about five years. She forced her envy away as she eyed the couple, the way Phillip looked into his wife's eyes—the same way Ryan used to look at Charlotte.

Pam seemed equally smitten. "Phillip is wonderful. He's in HR at a large CPA firm downtown."

Charlotte's friend had certainly done well for herself.

Phillip was taller than Pam with dark hair, handsome sharp features, and eyes as blue as Pam's. Charlotte briefly wondered if Phillip wore colored contacts too.

They settled into a comfortable conversation, and maybe it was the wine, or maybe it was Pam recalling some of their adventures in school, but Charlotte started to relax. All of her problems would still be there tomorrow, but for this night, she was going to enjoy herself. But she hoped Jacob was okay. She had charged her old cell phone and showed him how to use the Internet to make phone calls through apps that didn't require cellular service. Hopefully he was calling home and making amends with his family. Charlotte loved Jacob like a little brother, but he couldn't have shown up on her doorstep at a worse time.

Jacob kicked his feet up on Charlotte's coffee table and scanned the television channels. There was an entire channel that was nothing but documentaries about space and the universe. After about an hour of watching a narrator talk about the big bang theory, he landed on another show with the same name. Four smart young adults who had good jobs as scientists. They were funny, though, and Jacob didn't understand some of what they were saying, but it was fun to watch them interact with each other. He even laughed out loud, which was surprising, considering his circumstances. Jacob was thankful that Charlotte had stowed her dog in her bedroom. Little Buddy didn't seem to care for him. Jacob had never seen such a small animal carry on like that.

After a while, he turned down the volume on the television so he could think.

First he thought about Annie and hoped she was okay. Next, he thought about his parents, pictured his mother crying and saying, *"I knew this would happen."* Jacob felt a tiny level of comfort that they should have seen this coming, that it shouldn't be a shock, except maybe to Annie, the woman he'd promised to marry and take care of for the rest of her life.

Jacob had loved Annie since third grade, and he could still remember the first time she batted her eyes at him. It took him a few tries, but he was finally able to get a call to go through to her.

"I'm so sorry, Annie, about everything. I know you're hurting," he said when she answered. "And I know it's my fault." He paused, his heart beating fast. "But when the Lord calls us to a different life, we have to listen to Him. I came here because I felt real smothered there. Not by you or anything. I just knew I needed to be in a place where I could figure out some things, what my life purpose is."

"Your life *purpose*?"

Jacob clenched his jaw. He recognized the spitting anger in Annie's voice; he couldn't blame her.

"And what is your life *purpose*, Jacob?"

He'd practiced what he wanted to say, but this was tougher than he thought. "*Ach*, well . . . at first I just felt real trapped, like there was a world waiting for me to explore. But I loved you so much that I tried to make myself happy by staying. I do love you, Annie." He could hear her sniffling on the other end. "Please don't cry." Jacob dabbed at his eyes. He couldn't stand when Annie cried, and a few weeks ago, he would have done anything to prevent it. But now it was unavoidable. "I'm sorry," he whispered.

"I just don't understand." Annie's voice cracked between sobs. "Why would you say you want to marry me, then go and do this?"

Jacob blinked back tears. He'd taken the most cowardly way out possible. "I should have thought things through." He paused and took a long, deep breath. "I'm sorry, Annie."

Silence.

"Did you hear me, Annie?"

More silence.

"Annie?" he finally asked. "You there?"

After a few seconds, Jacob knew she'd hung up. He picked up the remote and tried to distract himself, but after a while, he found himself pacing and restless. He'd handled things badly with Annie. *Now what?*

Charlotte listened as Pam told Phillip about a time when she and Charlotte had put bubbles in a fountain at a nearby church.

"We were so scared we'd get caught," Pam said. "It was fairly harmless, but it was the worst thing either of us had ever done."

They all laughed, and Charlotte was glad that she'd been able to salvage some good memories from her childhood, even though they were mostly from her teenage years, at a time when she was old enough to take care of herself and not depend on her parents. During her last two years of high school, she'd lived with a friend's family. Ethan moved out that same year.

She excused herself to go to the ladies' room, toting her purse so she could touch up her lipstick. On her way back, she slowed her steps, then jolted to a halt when she saw him. *Ryan.*

He was sitting with a woman, and they were holding hands across the table. When he lifted the woman's hand to his mouth and kissed it, Charlotte's jaw dropped as adrenaline rushed from the tips of her toes to the top of her spinning head.

Ryan wasn't the type of man who moved into anything quickly, and it hadn't been long since they'd broken up. How was it that he had already worked into a relationship where hand kissing was allowed?

Charlotte's purse slid from her shoulder, and she left it there, hanging in the crook of her elbow. Maybe it was that action that triggered Ryan's attention, or maybe Charlotte had telepathically called him to look at her. Either way, Ryan's eyes met hers and widened as he sat taller. She forced herself to look away and headed back to her table, her heart racing. She'd pulled her purse back up on her shoulder and had barely gotten her breathing steady when she felt her purse vibrate.

She sat down, waited for the waiter to set their plates in front of them, then said, "Sorry. My purse is vibrating. I probably need to check this in case it's Jacob." She was sure it wasn't. Her hand trembled as she read Ryan's text.

This isn't what you think. She's a friend.

Charlotte shook as she typed in her own thoughts. She looks like more than a friend to me. But as her thumb hovered over the Send button, she thought about what she was doing. Maybe she should take the high road. She backspaced and retyped a new text. Enjoy your evening, Ryan. No worries on my end. I just want you to be happy.

Her thumb began to hover again, and as her heart thumped, she recalled how many times she'd apologized to Ryan. For checking his texts and phone calls . . . and ultimately heaving a candy dish across the room during one of their arguments. He'd left her feeling like all her hunches and gut feelings were wrong, that he and Shelley were just friends . . . and that Charlotte was a jealous girlfriend. She deleted the text again.

He was cheating on me after all. And that is probably Shelley sitting across the table from him. She picked at her food while Pam flagged down the waiter for water refills.

Charlotte wasn't going to feel peace until she knew one way or the other if the woman with Ryan was Shelley. If so, he'd lied about everything. Or at the very least, he'd wanted a relationship with Shelley, that is, if he wasn't already having one when he was with Charlotte.

"Can you guys excuse me again? Sorry." She nodded toward the back of the restaurant. "I thought I saw someone I know when I went to the restroom, and I'd like to go say hello if you don't mind." She hadn't mentioned anything about Ryan to Pam or Phillip, only that she wasn't seeing anyone at the moment. So it didn't make sense to explain now.

She eased out of her chair and walked in the direction of Ryan's table, her head held high. If the woman wasn't Shelley, Charlotte would be polite, introduce herself, and show Ryan that she wasn't a crazy, jealous lunatic. If it *was* Shelley, then she'd be polite, introduce herself, and show Ryan that she wasn't a crazy, jealous lunatic—and she'd walk away knowing she'd gotten the last word, both of them knowing Ryan hadn't been truthful with her.

She made her way in between tables, thankful she'd taken extra effort getting ready—including wearing Ryan's favorite perfume. Ryan blanched when he looked up and saw her standing at their table.

"Ryan, hello," she said in the sweetest voice she could

muster. She turned to the woman and extended her hand. "I'm Charlotte, a friend of Ryan's."

The woman finished swallowing whatever she had in her mouth and quickly cut her eyes in Ryan's direction before she looked back at Charlotte.

"Uh, hello. Nice to meet you, Charlotte." The woman's face began to mirror Ryan's in color as she shook Charlotte's hand. Even the best rouge couldn't hide her pallor. She was pretty, with her short brown hair cut in a sophisticated bob, shiny white teeth, and high cheekbones.

Charlotte fought the urge to scratch her eyes out. "And you are?" She blinked her eyes a few times but kept a smile on her face.

"Uh . . ." The woman glanced at Ryan again.

Ryan cleared his throat but didn't look at either woman when he said, "Charlotte, this is Shelley." Then it appeared that Ryan stopped breathing.

Charlotte's knees went weak, but she was determined to leave with her dignity intact. "Ryan, I just wanted to say hello, and . . ." She nodded once at Shelley. "It was nice to meet you, Shelley."

She forced herself to move slowly as she turned on her heel and headed back to her table, unable to eat most of her meal. Doing her best to stay vested in the conversation with Pam and Phillip, she was failing miserably and finally told Pam she wasn't feeling well.

Following promises to get together again soon,

Charlotte hurried toward the exit with an urgency that pulsed through her veins, tempting her to break into a sprint. Once she was outside the building, she leaned against the brick wall as cars whizzed by on the street. Tears started to come in earnest, and she didn't bother trying to keep them in. As she walked back to her car, she paused to type the most wretched text message she could come up with, filled with language that made her ashamed of herself. By the time she reached her car, she'd deleted the text again. But it took everything she had not to verbally rip him to shreds, the way he'd left her heart.

After the short drive home, she dried her tears as best she could before digging for her key at her apartment door.

"Jacob?" Charlotte pushed the door open. He wasn't on the couch. Buddy was barking wildly from her bedroom, so she rushed to let him out, kicking the bowl of water she'd left inside the room for him. "Jacob!"

It was a small apartment, so it didn't take long to conclude that he was gone.

She flopped onto the couch and noticed her pile of wadded-up tissues. As much as her heart hurt, she was worried about Jacob. He was a smart kid, or so she'd thought before today. But her Amish friend was far from street-smart.

Charlotte closed her eyes and leaned her head against the back of the couch. Buddy jumped in her lap, and after a few seconds of scratching behind his ears, she sat straight up and stiffened. Her eyes darted to the front door, where Jacob had left his suitcase when he arrived. The suitcase was no longer there.

She waited another three hours before she finally called Hannah.

"You lost him?" Hannah said after Charlotte explained.

"Well . . ." Charlotte squeezed her eyes shut, cringing. "I guess."

Three

Jacob trudged down the sidewalk as cars whizzed by him. A hazy fog hovered overhead as darkness fell on the city. He'd walked for so long, he'd gotten lost. Charlotte lived in a busy area of Houston, and apparently a fancy part of town. Jacob had gone to three hotels trying to get a room, but everything was over a hundred dollars per night, like Charlotte had said it would be.

He knew Charlotte would let him stay with her, but she had a lot going on. And his feelings were a little hurt that she hadn't been more welcoming. He'd spent nine dollars on a hamburger and french fries, and he'd given a man pushing a grocery cart five dollars. Now he was on the streets, walking with a heavy suitcase, unsure of anything in his life.

Charlotte was going to be worried sick, and the cell phone she'd given him wasn't working. Dead battery, he assumed. Maybe he hadn't thought this through well enough.

As he trudged along, he also thought about Annie. As much as he loved her, she didn't want the same life he did. He could make a fresh start here, but not walking in circles in an unfamiliar city. And he'd told Charlotte he'd help her pack her things.

He walked until he saw a business lit up on his right, flashing red lights that read Terry's Tattoos, so he pulled on the heavy glass door and walked inside. A cloud of cigarette smoke assaulted him and he fought the urge to cough. The place was loud, lots of buzzing, people sitting, lying down in chairs, and loud music blaring from every direction. He wanted to cover his ears.

"Hey! Look. An Amish kid."

Jacob turned in the direction of the voice. A man was sitting on a stool with a drill in his hand, rubbing it against another man's skin, a cigarette dangling from his lips. In a panic, Jacob looked around and saw lots of drills going. He'd seen a few tattoos on *Englisch* people before, but he'd never known this was how it was done. A large man with long blond hair, arms and neck covered in colorful designs, rose from a stool. Jacob couldn't understand why anyone would do that to their body, but when the man asked if Jacob was here to get a tattoo, he briefly considered it, something to signify his new adventure. But then the guy looked at Jacob's suitcase.

"Or are you running away, kid?"

Jacob cleared his throat as the man got closer, tempted to run. "*Nee.* I mean no." He realized right away it was a lie. Of course he'd run away. "I—I need to make a phone call. I need to call someone. I . . ."

Another man sitting nearby reached into the pocket of his blue jeans and pulled out a mobile phone. "Here, dude. Use my phone." Jacob set down his suitcase and walked to where the man was getting a colorful dragon painted onto his arm.

"*Danki*," he said and took the phone, keeping his eye on the dragon taking shape.

"I like your suspenders. Where you from, hon?" a pretty lady asked Jacob as he walked back to where he'd left his suitcase. She was the only woman in the place and didn't look like she belonged. She was getting something tattooed on her lower back.

"Lancaster County. In Pennsylvania," Jacob said as he tried to remember Charlotte's phone number. He'd memorized it before he left, but now he couldn't even recall the first digit.

"Pretty country there." The man who'd originally walked toward Jacob had sat down again and was back at work on an older man's arm. He nodded toward the counter with the cash register. "Hey, we got pizzas over there if you're hungry. Help yourself."

Jacob stared at the phone, searching his memory for Charlotte's number. It had been awhile since he'd had that hamburger. Annie always said he ate like he had a hole in his stomach. He moved toward the pizza boxes, carrying his suitcase. He stared at the pizzas covered in the one thing he didn't like—tomato sauce. But he was a little nervous in this place, and he didn't want to hurt these fellows' feelings, so he chose the smallest slice, then turned to the man who had loaned him the phone.

"I'm sorry. I'm having trouble remembering the number." Jacob wasn't sure whether to keep holding the phone or give it back.

"Maybe the person you're trying to call is listed. Just call information," the lady said through a puff of cigarette smoke. "Although, these days, lots of people only have a cell phone and no landline. But it's worth a shot."

Jacob wasn't sure how to do that. He searched the phone for an Information button.

"Here, hon. Bring it here." The woman waved a hand toward Jacob. Holding his pizza in one hand, he gave her the phone. "What's the name?" she asked.

"Uh . . . Charlotte." He forced himself to take a small bite of the pizza.

"Cutie pie, we're gonna need more than that." She grinned, and so did the man decorating her back with the drill. "Like a last name."

"Dol . . . um . . . Dolin—Dolinsky!" Jacob practically yelled it, and all at once he remembered Charlotte's phone number. "And I remember the number." He glanced around at all the friendly people, smiling and getting tattoos. One young man about Jacob's age seemed to have a bad cold. He snorted some sort of medicine up his nose. Another man began asking Jacob lots of questions about being Amish. Nothing he hadn't answered before. His town of Paradise was filled with curious tourists.

Someone turned the music way down, then they all started asking him questions. Nice, friendly folks. He was happy to talk with them. But he finally called Charlotte even though he'd had two offers of places to stay. The man with the cold had offered Jacob some of his medicine, but Jacob didn't feel sick, so he declined.

Charlotte was wide awake when her cell phone rang at ten thirty. She'd been praying Jacob would call, but when Terry's Tattoos flashed across the screen of her phone, she hit End and lay back down. *Jacob, where are you?* She'd talked to Hannah three times, and each time, she'd assured Jacob's sister that she was sure Jacob was fine, probably just decided to stay in a hotel somewhere. But Charlotte was doing enough worrying for all of them. Charlotte's apartment was in the Galleria area, and while it wasn't like being in downtown Houston, it wasn't the safest place to be at night. She jumped when her voice mail pinged with a new message.

"Oh no," she whispered as she listened.

She climbed out of bed, and a half hour later, she tapped on the locked glass door of Terry's Tattoos, relieved to see Jacob sitting in a chair next to his suitcase. A heavyset man with long blond hair moved toward the door. He was covered in tattoos and walked with a slight limp. Charlotte's heart thudded as she waited for the guy to unlock the door. She'd never visited any businesses on this street, and she had reasons for that. But she stepped across the threshold.

"*Wie bischt*, Charlotte." Jacob stood up quickly, picked up his suitcase, and was smiling ear to ear as he waved bye to the four people still in the tattoo shop. Three men were playing cards, and a woman in the corner puffed on a cigarette. "Bye, Terry." Jacob waved to the guy who'd unlocked the door, then he waved to the others. "Bye, Bruce and Lenny. And good luck with your husband, Cindy."

"You take care, hon," the woman said as she blew smoke. "Come back and see us anytime."

Charlotte held her breath, trying not to breathe in the secondhand smoke as she followed Jacob out of the place.

"Jacob!" It was all she could muster in a loud whisper as she opened the back passenger door for him to stow his suitcase. Luckily, this late at night, she'd been able to park right in front of the tattoo shop. She slammed the door, hurried to open the front passenger door, and practically shoved him in. *Stay calm*, she reminded herself as she hurried to the other side of the car, tires squealing as she peeled away. She momentarily saw the woman and child, heard the tires squealing in her head, but forced the thoughts away. "What were you thinking going into a place like that, especially this late at night? I've been worried sick. Your family and Annie have been worried too. Why did you leave my apartment?"

Jacob was gleaming, not the least bit upset. "It was an adventure. My first adventure in the city." He sat taller, then his expression shifted to something more serious, and in the darkness, it was hard to tell what he was thinking. "But I'm sorry I worried you."

"Well, you did, and you didn't answer my question. Why did you leave? I would have taken some time to show you around the next couple of days, before we head to Lancaster County." Charlotte had already made up her mind that she was moving to Pennsylvania. She had a house she owned free and clear—even if she wasn't sure she could live in it—and she wanted as far away from Ryan as she could get. Especially now that Jacob was okay, a visit to see her Amish friends would be a welcome relief. She'd sell Ethan's house and start fresh in Amish country.

"*Nee*, I'm not going back, but that doesn't mean you can't go for a visit. *Mamm*, *Daed*, and Hannah would love that."

"I'm not going for a visit," she said, raising her chin, proud that she was going to make a new start, stop all the crying, and get her life in order. "I'm moving there." Even in the dimly lit car, she saw Jacob's mouth fall open.

"Huh? Why would you want to live there?"

"It might be everything you're running away from, but I can't think of a better place to start fresh." She glanced his way when he didn't say anything. "Jacob, it costs a lot of money to live here. And once the newness of cars, televisions, and electricity wears off, I think you'll miss your old way of life."

He shrugged but fixed his eyes on the few people walking the streets. Charlotte quickly thanked God for keeping Jacob safe.

"You know what they say," she said as she made the last turn that led to her apartment complex. "The grass isn't always greener on the other side."

Jacob snapped his head to face her, his eyes wide. "Who says that?"

Charlotte waved a hand in his direction. "I don't know who said it first. It's just an expression. People always think things are better somewhere else, but they usually aren't."

"*Ach*, it's way better here."

She pulled into her parking space and waited for Jacob to get his suitcase. Once he was in step with her, she said, "I have a lot of packing to do, but I'll show you around some before we go back, okay?"

He nodded, which was a relief. When they'd gotten upstairs and were standing outside her door, Jacob grinned. "Look what I got."

Charlotte didn't look up at first, fumbling with the key in the lock, but after she'd pushed the door open and hit the light, she looked at him. She almost fell over the threshold when she saw his arm in the bright light of her apartment. "No, no, no," she said softly before she grabbed his wrist to get a better look at his arm. "Your mother is going to kill me." She leaned closer, pulling his short-sleeved shirt up his arm to see the tattoo in its entirety. "Forget your mother. Your father is going to kill me!" Charlotte dragged him into her apartment so hard that the suitcase fell from his hand as he stumbled inside. She slammed the door. Buddy was going nuts, barking and growling, but Charlotte didn't even try to shush him.

"Why did you *do* this?" Charlotte couldn't take her eyes off Jacob's arm. Up near his shoulder was a blue crescent moon with stars around it. It was mostly hidden by his shirtsleeve, but his Amish family was not going to approve of a tattoo. Charlotte squeezed her eyes closed as she clenched his wrist tighter and repeated herself. "Why, oh why?"

Jacob frowned, but only briefly as he wiggled out of Charlotte's grasp. Then his face lit up again. "I don't know why you're upset. Cindy said it would be cool to have a moon and stars on my arm since I like space stuff."

She could have sworn he'd been wearing a long-sleeved shirt when he arrived. "Did you change shirts?" It should have been the last thing on her mind, but keeping his arm covered would become a priority soon.

"*Ya.* Terry asked me to take off my shirt so he could do the tattoo, but I ain't real . . . muscular. So I put on a short-sleeved shirt I had in my suitcase and just rolled up the sleeve."

Charlotte walked to her couch and fell onto it, her purse still in her hands. She laid her head back as she kicked off her flip-flops and lowered her eyelids. After a few moments, she opened one eye. Jacob was still standing right inside the door, and even though Buddy wasn't barking anymore, he was growling and hopping from one side to the other every time Jacob tried to take a step.

"Is your dog gonna bite me?"

"Maybe." Charlotte grinned, then called Buddy to her. Once he was beside her on the couch, she reached into her purse and dug around for her phone, noticing it was eleven thirty. Hannah had said to call, no matter what time it was, if Charlotte heard from Jacob. She scrolled through her contacts until she found the number and was about to hit Call when she looked at Jacob, who'd finally made it into the living room.

"He's here," she said when Hannah answered after the first ring. "And he's fine. I'll show him around Houston, and then he can come with me to Lancaster County in a few days." Charlotte smiled, then explained her decision to move there. Despite her evening, she loved hearing Hannah's excitement, both that Jacob was all right and that Charlotte was relocating. "Yep. That's right. As soon as I can get packed, rent a U-Haul, and handle my affairs, Jacob and I will be driving there."

She glanced up at Jacob, who was shaking his head and whispering, "I'm not going back."

She covered the mouthpiece of her cell phone, mouthing back, "Yes, you are."

After she hung up, she took a deep breath and let it out slowly, yawning. "I'll get you some blankets for the couch. We need to get to sleep. I have tons of packing to do, some work stuff to finish, and a whole bunch of phone calls to make." She yawned again as Jacob walked to one of the wicker chairs and sat down, Buddy growling.

"Charlotte . . . ," he said softly.

She waited, emotionally and physically exhausted. But packing to move and starting fresh would help keep her mind off of Ryan, even though punching him in the nose sounded almost as good as clawing Shelley's eyes out, neither of which she'd really do.

"I'm not going back." Jacob sat a little taller.

Charlotte sighed, hoping things would look different to him in the morning.

Four

Annie buried her face in her hands as Hannah and Lena sat on either side of her on the couch. She knew Jacob's sister and mother were as upset as she was. Annie's mother paced the living room as Annie's brother, Daniel, stood nearby with his arms folded across his chest. Annie wasn't sure where her father was.

"I understand that Charlotte will be moving here, but why is Jacob planning to stay in Texas? He won't know anyone there," Annie asked for the third time. "And I don't understand why Charlotte is helping him by letting him stay in her apartment until the end of the month." She uncovered her face, her hands flailing in the air. Annie didn't really know Charlotte. She'd only been around the woman a few times. But she knew Charlotte's background. She'd lied to Jacob's family, pretending to be Amish so that she could find out why her brother had committed suicide. Jacob's family had found out about Charlotte and chosen to forgive her. The *Englisch* woman had even let Jacob's mother, Lena, stay with her, and had taken her for cancer treatments in Houston. But Annie didn't trust Charlotte or anyone who was helping to keep Jacob away from her.

Lena patted Annie's leg, then slowly lifted herself off the couch. "Charlotte said she was going to continue to try to change his mind up until the time she leaves. But if he refuses to leave Texas, hon, Charlotte can't drag him home by his hair. He'll at least have a safe place to stay until the end of the month."

Hannah stood up also, and when Annie's mother finally stopped pacing, the three women stood looking down at Annie while Daniel leaned against the far wall, arms still folded across his chest.

"I'm sure Jacob will come to his senses and come home soon," Lena said in a shaky voice.

Annie wasn't sure of anything anymore. A few days ago, she was planning to marry Jacob, Lena was her future mother-in-law, and Hannah would have been her sister-in-law. Now her husband-to-be was in Houston, having taken leave of his senses. *Or maybe he just doesn't love me enough.* She eased herself up from the couch and draped an arm across her stomach, sniffling.

Lena and Hannah both hugged her good-bye, then Annie's mother walked with them to their buggy. Annie watched them from the window. Lena started to cry, and Hannah wrapped an arm around her. She glanced over her shoulder at Daniel, who hadn't moved, a frown sprawling across his face. Daniel was usually outspoken, but he hadn't said a word since he found out Jacob had left.

She stared at her brother until he finally said, "What?"

Annie groaned. "You haven't said anything."

Daniel lowered his arms and shrugged. "What do you want me to say?" He stopped glaring at her, but his gray eyes darkened.

"Why are you looking at me like that?" Annie expected sympathy from her older brother, but maybe he was so angry with Jacob that he couldn't be compassionate right now. "He's the one that left, but you're looking at me like it's my fault." *Maybe it is.* She searched her mind, but she couldn't recall a time when she and Jacob had ever had more than a mild disagreement. Nothing to justify his leaving like this.

Daniel shrugged again. "I didn't say it was your fault."

Annie huffed as she slammed her hands to her hips. "I didn't do anything to run him off, if that's what you're wondering. He just left! Left me. Left . . ." She stopped and glanced out the window again. Her mother, Lena, and Hannah were all still talking. Maybe they were wondering the same thing—what Annie had done to run off Jacob.

"Who else did he leave, Annie?" Daniel kept his eyes locked on hers as he moved closer. Her only brother was a tall man with broad shoulders. He was eight years older than her, and he'd been protecting her for her entire life. But now, as his shadow cast darkness the length of her, he showed an emotion she couldn't quite identify. Daniel's lip twitched, the way it did when he was really upset.

"What—what do you mean?" Annie shook off the threatening tears.

Daniel stepped closer to her. "You said that Jacob left *us*, that he left *you*, that he left . . ." He waved an arm in the air. "Who else?"

Annie didn't think she had any tears left, but as she crossed an arm over her belly, a tear slipped down her cheek. She lowered her head, then covered her face and sobbed. Daniel finally pulled her into a hug and kissed the top of her head. "*Mei maedel*," he whispered. Annie was glad to hear sympathy in his voice, but any comfort she felt was short-lived and replaced with fear. She eased away but looked him in the eye.

"Are you going to tell?" Her voice squeaked, and she fought a growing panic.

Daniel stared at her stomach but didn't say anything.

"How long have you known?" Shame wrapped around her like a thick wet blanket, and she wished the floor would just swallow her up.

"I remember when *Mamm* was pregnant with you. She threw up a lot in the mornings." Daniel rubbed his forehead before he looked back at her. "And if you're going to take a pregnancy test like the *Englisch* folks, you shouldn't leave the empty box in plain view in the bathroom trash can."

Annie held her breath. Daniel had been through a rough patch of his own a few years ago, when he and Edna Glick had broken up, but she couldn't recall seeing him this upset since then. "Are you going to tell *Mamm* and *Daed*? I'll be shunned."

"You're only seventeen years old, and you and Jacob should have known better." Daniel's face reddened as he pointed at her.

Sobs racked her insides, and a tear trickled down her cheek before she could stop it. Annie recalled the liberties she and Jacob had taken, things they'd done that weren't right in the eyes of God. They'd only done it once, and afterward they'd agreed it wouldn't happen again until after they were married. She glanced out the window again and wished she could be in two places at once.

"And *nee*, *Mamm* and *Daed* don't know," Daniel said. "I've been waiting for you to tell them—or for Jacob to tell them. But he ran out on you, leaving you to handle this on your own. Jacob wasn't raised like that. And I know he's only a few months older than you, but if he's old enough to get my baby sister pregnant, he's old enough to be a man about it."

Annie's knees were weak, her stomach roiling, and

her heart was beating way too fast. She opened her mouth to respond, but nothing came out.

"Jacob's a coward," Daniel said, stomping his foot on the wood floor hard enough to rattle the dishes in the china cabinet. He looked over her shoulder and sighed. "*Mamm*'s coming back in. You're going to have to tell her soon."

"Not now," she managed to say. "Please, Daniel. Not today. I'll tell them soon. When Jacob comes back, we can tell our parents together, even if it does mean we'll be shunned."

"*If* Jacob comes back. You don't know if he will. What kind of man leaves the woman he loves, especially when she's carrying his child?"

Annie heard footsteps on the porch, and in a whisper she said, "Jacob doesn't know. He doesn't know about the baby."

~

Daniel froze, but he forced his shoulders to relax when his mother walked back into the living room. *Mamm*'s eyes were red and swollen like Hannah's and Lena's had been, and the way Annie's were too.

"Come, come," *Mamm* said, and she put an arm around Annie, guiding her toward the kitchen. "Hot tea and a slice of banana nut bread will do us both some good."

Annie put a hand over her mouth, her shoulders slumped. Daniel wondered if she was going to vomit, but they disappeared into the kitchen. He walked out onto the front porch and took a deep breath. It had been a long day filled with crying women. As dusk began to settle over the Byler household, Daniel believed the darkness would lift in the morning, making way for a new day. But he feared what the future held, especially for Annie.

In the distance, he could see his father coming in from the far barn. Any hint of snow was gone, melted by the afternoon sun, but the air was damp and cool for March. He shivered as he waited for his father. Daniel had assumed he would wed before Annie, and it was a little embarrassing that he hadn't found someone yet to share his life with. He'd stopped trying very hard after his breakup with Edna.

But he wanted Annie to be happy, and it wasn't her fault that Daniel remained unmarried at twenty-five. He'd be the oldest bachelor in their district once Isaac married Hannah in the fall. Daniel's best chance at love had fallen apart, but Edna was married to John Dienner now, and there was no point looking back.

He wanted to tell his father about Annie, hoping his parents would make wise decisions for his sister, but ultimately the choices wouldn't be Annie's. There was a chance Annie would be shunned. Even if their parents didn't push the issue, the bishop and deacons might, in an effort to make Annie see the error of her ways. But no matter the circumstances, a child would be born, and that was a gift from God. Daniel wondered if he would ever receive that blessing.

"Any more news about Jacob?" Lucas Byler strode across the yard, his broad shoulders pulled back. Pride was looked down upon, but his father carried himself like a proud man, even though he was generally quiet, especially if trouble was brewing. It was his mother who handled family situations, and while that was unusual in their community, it seemed to work for his parents.

"*Nee.* Just that he will be staying at Charlotte's apartment in the city until the end of the month." Daniel shared Annie's opinion about that. Why was Charlotte helping the boy, making it easy for him to stay away?

Daed shook his head as he moved past Daniel and went into the house. "And then what?"

"I don't know." Daniel stayed outside, rethinking things. His conclusion was that his parents wouldn't send Annie away, not pregnant with their grandchild. If Jacob came back and quickly married Annie, the bishop may be lenient.

Daniel clenched his fists. He'd always liked Jacob, but right now he was praying for the Lord to help him shed his anger toward the boy. And that Jacob would do the right thing.

~

Annie got into bed, placed her arms across her belly, and wondered what Jacob's reaction would be to her being pregnant. They'd gone against what they knew was right by making a baby before they were married, and she'd been praying about that, but she couldn't help but be excited about becoming a mother. A tiny new life was growing inside her.

Tears filled her eyes as the tree outside her window shimmied against a moonlit night, tiny starbursts dancing on the ceiling above her head. She wondered what Jacob was thinking and finally let the tears come. The man she loved had left her. She was unwed and pregnant. And terrified about what her parents would say and do when they found out. Annie had always known that Jacob was fascinated by the outside world, but she'd thought their love would be enough to make up for it. He'd chosen his own wants and needs over hers. Daniel's words rang in her head—*Jacob's a coward.* She wondered if Jacob would have left if he'd known she was pregnant.

~

It took Charlotte a week to finish packing. Jacob helped, and in exchange Charlotte kept her promise and showed him around Houston, mostly doing things that didn't cost much money. They'd worked in the mornings and part of the afternoons, then traveled around sightseeing for two or three hours. The Waterwall Park was only a few miles from Charlotte's apartment, and Jacob loved watching the sixty-four-foot semicircular fountain that recirculated eleven thousand gallons of water per minute. They'd visited a couple of museums, and on the last day, they knocked off work early and went to Galveston since Jacob had never seen the ocean or been to the beach. For Charlotte the activities had felt like a farewell tour of the only life she'd ever known.

"You know you have to be out of my apartment by the end of the day on March 31, right?" she asked again as they walked to the parking lot of her apartment. "That's only six days from now."

"*Ya*. I know. I'm waiting on phone calls—two places about a job and three about an apartment."

Charlotte stopped in front of the U-Haul she'd rented and hoped Jacob would have better luck securing an apartment than she did. Credit scores were *the* determining factor these days of how financially stable you were, and Charlotte's rating had slipped over the past year. She doubted Jacob had much of a score at all. She'd sold her car just the day before, pawned a few things earlier in the week, and Jacob and the kid down the hall—Benny—had loaded all of her furniture except for the couch. Jacob needed something to sleep on, and Pam and Phillip had offered to buy it after Charlotte explained her plans to them. It would have been a tight squeeze to get it in the moving van anyway. She loved that couch, one of the only things she'd ever really splurged on in her life, but Charlotte needed the cash.

She pointed to Jacob's pocket where she knew he kept his cell phone. "That phone I had turned on for you doesn't have a lot of minutes, so keep that in mind. If and when you get a job, you can always add more." She'd been praying Jacob would change his mind and go to Lancaster County with her, but he hadn't budged. She wrapped her arms around his neck and kissed him on the cheek, then she looked at the truck again and sighed. "Wish me luck." She'd never driven anything bigger than a pickup truck, and this baby was massive.

Jacob smiled. "I'll do better than that. I'll pray you have a safe trip."

Charlotte opened the door, threw her purse inside, and climbed into the high seat, trusting that Jacob's strong faith would guide him and keep him safe.

"Happy Easter in two days." Jacob barely lifted the corners of his mouth. It was surely the first Easter he'd ever spent alone.

After a final good-bye, Charlotte put the truck in gear and inched forward to start her new life. It was possible to make it to the heart of Amish country by Easter Sunday, but Charlotte didn't foresee reaching Paradise, Pennsylvania, by then. She planned to take things nice and slow. She'd spent plenty of Easters alone in the past. But sadness wrapped around her as she looked in her rearview mirror at Jacob standing in the parking lot of what used to be her home.

"Godspeed, my friend," she whispered. "And be safe."

She wasn't even out of Houston when her phone buzzed, and she knew better than to let her cell phone distract her while she was driving this big rig, so she waited until she was stopped at a red light on the feeder of the freeway before she looked at the text message—from Ryan.

Just checking on you. I hope you're doing okay.

Charlotte stared at the words for a few moments. *Words.* That's all they were. She deleted the text. Then deleted his contact information. And got back on the road.

Five

Daniel still had trouble seeing Edna and John together, but unless he moved to another district, he couldn't avoid seeing them every other Sunday at worship service and randomly around town. He wanted Edna to be happy, but he still didn't understand why she'd married John. Daniel had been dating Edna for almost a year when she started to distance herself. But even this morning at Easter worship, Edna didn't look happy. She didn't smile much, and she looked tired, or like her eyes were swollen from crying. She'd looked that way earlier when he'd run into them at the hardware store. Daniel was glad to be back home, glad that his chores were done for the day. He was going to take a long nap, something he rarely did.

As he made his way down the hallway upstairs, he heard Annie whimpering from behind her closed bedroom door. He told himself to keep walking. His sister had looked a lot like Edna today with bags under her tired eyes, and Daniel was sure that Annie hadn't cracked a smile all day. Annie had plenty to be upset about, and a part of Daniel wanted to pound Jacob into the ground. He'd only taken a few steps past Annie's room when he turned around and tapped lightly on her door.

"Annie?"

"I don't want to talk, Daniel."

He rubbed his chin, tempted to go take his nap, but he pushed the door open. Annie was sitting on the bed with a box of tissues next to her and a blanket across her lap. It was chilly inside, and Daniel hoped this was the last of the cold weather before spring. He sat down on the bed beside her.

"I know you're hurting, *mei maedel*." Daniel wasn't sure whether to pray for Jacob to come back or not. The lad was young, but what Jacob had done was dishonorable. What kind of husband would he be? "Soon you will have to tell *Mamm* and *Daed* that you are with child, whether or not Jacob chooses to come back."

"He's not coming back," Annie said through her tears as she reached for another tissue.

"You've talked to him?"

"*Ya.* He called a little while ago." She covered her face with her hands, sobbing harder.

Daniel waited a few moments, but when he couldn't find anything good to say about Jacob, he stayed quiet.

Annie uncovered her face and sniffled. "He is happy to be starting a new life, a life that doesn't include me." She folded her hands across her stomach. "Or our child."

Daniel stared at her, narrowing his eyebrows. "Did you tell him about the baby?"

"*Nee.* I'm not going to trap him. I don't want him coming back just because I'm pregnant."

"Seems to be a *gut* enough reason to me, to do the honorable thing."

Annie started to cry again, so Daniel sat quietly, not wanting to upset her more. Despite the coolness of the room, beads of sweat gathered on his forehead. He didn't like seeing his sister like this, and the more he thought about it, the angrier he became. "Why did Charlotte let him stay in her apartment when she is on her way here?" Daniel still had trouble referring to the *Englisch* woman as Charlotte since she'd used the name Mary Troyer when she was deceiving everyone last year.

"I'm not sure. The point is . . . he doesn't want to be with me. If he wasn't staying at Charlotte's home in the city, he'd just stay somewhere else." She sniffled, glancing at her stomach.

"Maybe. But I don't trust Charlotte. Who knows how she might have influenced his decisions. Maybe you're better off without Jacob, that scoundrel."

"Don't call him that. He's the man I love, the father of my child." She covered her face again, weeping. Daniel draped his arm over her shoulder and pulled her closer.

But Annie eased away from him when they heard footsteps in the hallway. Heavy footsteps. Daniel couldn't remember the last time his father had come upstairs for anything. He had a bad knee, so the stairs were troublesome for him.

Annie dabbed at her tears, then scooped up all her used tissues and hid them under the blanket in her lap. "It sounds like *Daed*, and I don't want him to see me crying."

As he glanced at his sister's swollen, red eyes, Daniel figured it was too late for that, but he didn't say anything. Someone tapped on the door twice. "Annie?"

"*Ya*, come in."

Daed limped over the threshold, his right leg bent slightly at the knee. Stroking his beard, *Daed*'s eyebrows furrowed. Daniel took a deep breath and held it, wondering if their parents had found out Annie was with child.

"I'm glad you're here, too, Daniel." Their father staggered to the rocking chair in the corner and lowered himself into it, keeping his right leg extended, his face tightened with strain. Daniel wondered why he hadn't just called them downstairs.

"Your mother was not up to talking right now. The Easter festivities have taken a toll on her. But I see that you've been crying, Annie, so you must already know what I'm about to say."

This is it. Annie is going to get shunned. Daniel couldn't believe it.

"I understand we're going to have a new life in our

family." *Daed* sighed, and Daniel quickly looked at Annie. His sister was blinking back tears.

"*Daed*—" was all Annie was able to choke out before her sobs took over.

"There, there, *mei maedel*," their father said as his own eyes watered. "We will all get through this together. It is not the most ideal situation, that's for sure." He shook his head. "I'm told that at this age, childbirth can be difficult."

Annie cried harder. *Daed* cleared his throat. "But we will do everything we can to make sure your mother has the best doctors to help her through this."

Daniel stopped breathing. "*Mamm* is pregnant." He tried to say the words so it didn't sound like a question, since their father had already said that a new life was coming into their family. *Daed* nodded. "She's *fifty-two*," Daniel whispered. He didn't even know it was possible to get pregnant at that age.

"A baby is a blessing, no matter the circumstances." Their father latched onto the arms of the rocker and lifted himself out of the chair. "When the Lord sees fit to send us the gift of a child, we must be thankful and obedient."

Daniel glanced at Annie, who also seemed to be holding her breath.

I hope you still think that when you find out about Annie.

Charlotte stepped out of the cab of the U-Haul and called Buddy to follow. He scurried over the console, then jumped from the seat into the grass. Charlotte breathed in the Lancaster County air while she waited for Buddy to do his business, then trudged through the yard toward the wraparound porch that surrounded the King homestead. She pulled her sweater snug with one hand, carrying her small red suitcase with the other as Buddy hopped along behind her.

With tired legs and a heavy heart, she mastered the steps and knocked on the front door, surprised that no one had come out to greet her. She heard someone clomping down the stairs, and seconds later Hannah opened the door.

Charlotte smelled the wonderful aroma of freshly baked bread just before Hannah jumped into her arms. "I'm so glad you're here. I've missed you!" Hannah gave her a final squeeze, eased away, and glanced over Charlotte's shoulder, an easy task since Hannah was quite a bit taller than Charlotte. "I can't believe you drove that big truck all the way here." Then she leaned down and ran a hand along Buddy's back. "Welcome to our home, Buddy."

"I wish I could have made it by yesterday for Easter, but I was exhausted. And Hannah, I tried everything to get Jacob to change his mind. He said if he couldn't stay at my place, that he would leave, but that he wasn't going home. And believe me, he is safer at my place than he is walking the streets of Houston, since he hasn't secured an apartment or a job yet." She recalled the two hours she'd spent talking to Jacob, trying to convince him to come with her. "He knows he has to be out of my apartment by the end of the month, which is in a few days." She was wishing Hannah would invite her in so they could discuss it over a slice of buttered bread. "But he's fine, and at least we know where he is . . . for now."

Hannah finally stepped aside so Charlotte and Buddy could go inside. It seemed weird to have a fire in the fireplace when it had been so hot in Houston, but it was toasty warm in the living room and a relief from the chill outside.

"We will just continue to pray for our Jacob." Hannah took Charlotte's suitcase and carried it to the landing near the stairs. Charlotte warmed her hands by the fire until Hannah motioned for them to take a seat on the couch. Buddy curled up on a rug in front of the fireplace as if he'd lived there forever.

"I thought if maybe he had a few days alone, he'd come to realize that this is where he needs to be. Houston is a busy, loud place, especially where I live. I just can't imagine he'd be happy there for long. And I brought my television, so I think he is going to be bored." She looked around. She'd been nervous about facing Amos, but she was disappointed that Lena wasn't home. "Where are your parents?"

"They send their regrets that they couldn't be here to

greet you, but they went over to the Bylers' *haus* to visit with Annie, Daniel, and their parents." Hannah shook her head. "As if they don't have enough to deal with, Jacob leaving and all, they just found out that Eve is pregnant. Do you remember Daniel and Annie's mother, Eve?"

Charlotte nodded. "I was only around the Byler family a few times, but I remember them."

Hannah pressed her lips into a frown. "Eve is fifty-two," Hannah whispered, glancing around as if someone might hear.

"Um, yikes. A bit risky at her age."

Hannah folded her hands in her lap, just as beautiful as she'd always been with her dark hair and striking features. Charlotte had often pictured what Hannah would look like with makeup on, but she didn't need any.

Charlotte thought about the weeks she'd spent in this house pretending to be Mary Troyer in an effort to find out what happened to her brother, Ethan. She regretted the lies. But she'd found God here, and Hannah and her family. Through her sins, she'd come to know a better way of life. But she didn't understand why God gave her glimpses of happiness but never anything solid to hold on to. Maybe she hadn't earned happiness yet.

"I want to hear everything about you and Ryan." Hannah reached for Charlotte's hand and squeezed. "But first, I need you to tell me more about Jacob. *Mamm* is very upset. We all are, but I think she's taking it the hardest. And I don't think Annie is doing very well either."

Charlotte fought a yawn, longing for a piece of buttered bread but not wanting to mention it.

"Jacob said that he loves Annie, but he feels like he doesn't belong here." Charlotte paused, not wanting to be hurtful but feeling the need to stay completely truthful. "Hannah . . ." She took a deep breath. "I could be wrong about this, but . . ."

Hannah stiffened. "What?"

"I just can't help but wonder if maybe Annie isn't the one for Jacob. I mean, if he loves her so much, why didn't he ask her to move with him? I asked Jacob about that, and he said he could never pull Annie from here. But"—Charlotte shrugged—"how could he leave her?"

Hannah stared out the window, then refocused on Charlotte. "I've wondered the same thing. We've all known that Jacob seemed to need more learning than the rest of us. He was always reading books and talking about things we didn't understand. But we thought for sure that once he'd asked Annie to marry him, he'd stay." Hannah shook her head. "Seventeen is so young."

Too young to make life decisions, but the Amish married young. Charlotte was glad that by the time Hannah married Isaac, Hannah would be almost twenty-six, although that was practically an old maid by Amish standards. Charlotte would be almost twenty-eight by then. Queen of the old maids in Amish terms.

"Jacob has never been alone," Charlotte said, trying to infuse some hope into her voice. "Maybe after being by himself in my apartment for a while, he'll realize how wonderful it is here and want to come back. He'll start to miss y'all and realize that the hustle and bustle of Houston isn't for him. And maybe realize he's meant to be with Annie." She bit back tears, determined not to cry. She'd had plenty of time to think about herself and Ryan during her commute, but she pushed the thoughts away now.

"I had an old cell phone, so I added Jacob to my account, for now. But he doesn't have many minutes. I didn't like the idea of him not having a way to communicate with us, and just using apps via the Internet seemed confusing for him." *Please, God, keep him safe.*

Hannah sighed. "Okay. *Danki.* I'm not sure I understand all that, but it was nice of you to help Jacob." She folded her hands in her lap. "Now, about you. I'm so glad you chose to stay at our house until Ethan's house sells."

Charlotte glanced at Buddy, who'd fallen asleep. "Are you sure it's okay with your parents that I brought my dog?" She was already unsure where her relationship stood with Amos, and Buddy nipping at his legs wasn't going to go well.

"Of course." Hannah nodded toward the window at the big U-Haul truck. "What's next? Do you want me to get Isaac and some others to store your things at Ethan's house?"

Charlotte let out a long breath. "I, uh . . . need to talk to you about that. I contacted a real estate agent, and we got the house listed via e-mail, but she suggested that I not put a bunch of boxes and such at the house, that it will show better empty." She bit her bottom lip. "Do you think it would be okay to store my things in your basement until the house sells and I find a place to live?"

Hannah smiled. "Charlotte, I can see that you are exhausted, but this is one thing you shouldn't worry about. *Ya*, we will get your things stored in our basement. And we will enjoy you being here for as long as you'd like."

"Thank you." Charlotte felt weird. Things were moving too fast. She reminded herself that she was just as strong and capable as the next person. She wasn't going to allow herself to slip into overload, so she redirected the conversation. "How are the wedding plans coming?"

Hannah's features lit up and her eyes twinkled. "*Gut*. Very *gut*. Isaac and I can't wait."

Charlotte fought back more tears as she thought about Ryan. "Well, you just bask in your happiness with Isaac and don't let this little snafu with Jacob upset you too much. If he chooses not to come back, you might have to just accept that."

"He'll come back. He will miss Annie." The corners of her lips rose. "And us."

~

Jacob stared at himself sideways in the full-length mirror in the bathroom. If he flexed his arm a certain way, he could make his tattoo move a little, which made him chuckle. It looked like the moon was tipping to one side and spilling stars. He studied his profile some more, wishing he wasn't so skinny. His body size didn't reflect his ability to do hard work. Sighing, he pulled on a pair of his black slacks and a blue shirt he'd brought from home, deciding to leave it untucked. And no suspenders. He wished he had some *Englisch* clothes, but if a hamburger and fries cost nine dollars, he figured he'd better save what he had left to secure a place to live. But so far, no word on an apartment and no return calls about jobs he'd applied for. Jacob wasn't a liar, but he'd hesitated when filling out applications. Each one asked for the amount of schooling he'd had. The *Englisch* went to school until they were eighteen, then often to college. Jacob, as with all Amish kids, had only been schooled until he was fourteen. He wondered if that was why he wasn't getting any job interviews. If he didn't have a job in a few days, he'd have to go to a hotel, and his money wouldn't last long unless he could find a really cheap one.

As he made his way to the kitchen, his stomach growled.

He took out a gallon of tea. It came ready-made from the market, and it wasn't nearly as good as the meadow tea back home. He chugged it straight from the bottle, wishing Charlotte had sodas instead. *Mamm* didn't think sodas were healthy, so she never bought any.

He put the tea back and scanned the food that was

left. Charlotte had left her groceries, and all he had to do was clean out her refrigerator and pantry before he left. Her friends would be by to pick up her couch. *Mamm* wouldn't have approved of a lot of the things Charlotte kept on hand. Cheese that came in a package and powdered creamer. There were pickles in a jar, which he'd already tried, not the same as the ones *Mamm* made. He would need to quit comparing everything to how it was at home, and over time he was sure he'd get used to things here. But as he eyed what was left in the refrigerator, he wondered again why there weren't any fresh fruits or vegetables. There were packages of deli meats, four jars of mayonnaise, each with only a little bit left—and he still didn't understand why Charlotte kept her bread in the refrigerator.

He opened the freezer. *Now, this is better.* He reached for the strawberry shortcake ice cream, and thankfully the container was half full. Charlotte seemed to eat a lot of ice cream before she left. He spotted some frozen french fries and some little boxes that looked like ready-to-go meals for the microwave. Ready in only a few minutes. He wondered how good a meal in a box could be. He hadn't been brave enough to try one yet.

Jacob found a spoon and headed toward the living room, the feel of the beige carpet tickling his bare feet. Once he got settled and said a prayer, he dug into the ice cream as the hum of the air-conditioning kept the apartment a cool seventy degrees. How he longed for a television though.

He reached for one of the books Charlotte had left in a pile on the floor, and as he did, he dropped a huge spoonful of reddish-pink ice cream on Charlotte's white couch.

By the time he found a towel, wet it, and returned to the living room, the ice cream had mostly melted into a huge blob. He scrubbed and scrubbed, but with each effort, the spot got bigger. Charlotte's white couch absorbed it like a sponge, until the dollop had turned into a messy patch of pink the size of a small kitchen plate.

He could think of only two people who might be able to help him. His mother. And Annie. He sure couldn't ask Charlotte what to do.

Annie stared at her cell phone buzzing on her nightstand. Her parents had agreed to let her keep it on, but only on the vibrate mode. She considered not answering Jacob's call, but maybe he was calling to say he'd made a terrible mistake, that he was coming home and they'd all be a family.

"I'm in a heap of trouble," Jacob said when she answered. Annie's heart pounded and she brought a hand to her chest.

"Are you okay? Have you been in an accident?"

"I spilled red ice cream on Charlotte's white couch. It's bad, all mushed into the fabric. I tried to clean it, but I just made it worse! I don't know what to do. And I can't ask Charlotte. I think she'd be mad I let this happen. Maybe not. But I'd like to just not tell her. What should I use to get it clean?"

Annie was too shocked to answer.

"You still there? What should I do?"

"Jacob . . ."

"*Ya?*"

"I'm so glad that you thought to call me about something this important." She pressed her lips together so tightly she thought they might be stuck that way.

"You were the first person I thought of. Well, you and *Mamm*." His voice reflected his pride at having thought of her, which only fueled her anger.

"I bet it's a nasty stain, all that red on a white couch."

"*Ach*, it's awful, Annie. I wonder what a couch like this costs."

"Probably thousands of dollars," she said, smiling now.

"*Nee! Nee*. What should I do?"

Annie tapped a finger to her chin. "Hmm . . . let me think a minute." *Let's see. You left me without notice, alone and pregnant. And yet I'm the one you casually call about cleaning a couch?* "Still thinking," she added.

"Thank you for helping me, Annie. I thought you might be mad. It's just . . ." He breathed heavily into the phone. "I never saw God's plan for me. If I had, I wouldn't have asked you to marry me. I love you. I really do."

Annie wilted into her bedcovers, where she'd been most of the day. She'd told her mother she was sick to her stomach, which was true, even if she hadn't admitted knowing why. She wondered if her mother was having morning sickness too. But mostly, she hung on Jacob's words, hoping they were a prelude to his saying he would come home. If he loved her, surely that meant more than anything else. "I love you too, Jacob."

"Great. So how do I get this stain out?" His chipper voice returned, and Annie was sure she was going to hurl.

"Hmm . . . ," she said, returning to her original train of thought. "Here's what you do . . ." *You jerk.* "Go find where Charlotte keeps her cleaning supplies, maybe under the kitchen counter."

"Okay. She took most everything with her in the moving truck, but I'll go look and see what she's got."

Annie could hear him rustling around. She sat up and folded her legs underneath her, suddenly feeling much better. "Did you find anything?"

"*Ya, ya.* She must have forgotten this stuff or didn't think she'd need it."

"Read me what she has."

"Uh . . . She's got Windex, Pine-Sol, something called a Magic Eraser, 409, Pledge . . . uh, some sponges, Palmolive, and . . . a canning jar with a sticker that says Bacon Grease on it, and—"

"That's it. Take out the bacon grease . . . and what color is the Pine-Sol?" *God, forgive me.*

"The Pine-Sol is purple. I'm going to read the instructions first."

"*Nee, nee.* Don't do that. Just get a bowl and mix a cup of bacon grease with two tablespoons of the Pine-Sol." Annie put a hand over her mouth for a few seconds. "And make sure it's mixed really well. Oh, and you'll need those Magic Eraser things too."

Despite the laughter that threatened to erupt, she couldn't go through with this. It was an evil thing to do, and no matter what Jacob had done, it was no reason to ruin Charlotte's couch. She shook her head, smiling. "Jacob, maybe that's not—"

"Annie, thank you so much for helping me," he interrupted. "Charlotte told me men don't know how to clean, and she was right. Hey, Charlotte should be there by now. Have you seen her yet? Whatever you do, don't tell her about this. I'll fix it, and she'll never know. That isn't a lie. I'm just not going to tell her. I feel like Charlotte would forgive me, but I'd rather she didn't know about it."

Charlotte, Charlotte, Charlotte. Annie stiffened to the point she felt like she might break in two if she heard that woman's name one more time. "I don't know if *Charlotte* has arrived yet." She cleared her throat. "Anyway, mix the Pine-Sol with the grease. Apply it directly to the spot on the couch, and—"

"On her white couch? Is this some sort of miracle potion? It sounds weird."

Annie took a deep breath and slowly let it out, her best effort not to laugh. "Now, Jacob. You admitted you don't know how to clean. Just pour the entire bowlful on the couch, then you'll want to use the Magic Eraser to scrub the spot as hard as you can."

"*Ach*, that must be the miracle part—*Magic* Eraser." He laughed. "*Danki*, Annie. You're the best. I can't find a bowl, but Charlotte left some paper plates and plastic cups for me to use. Will a plastic cup work?"

"*Ya*. That should work mighty fine."

"*Danki* again, Annie."

"You're more than welcome, Jacob."

She snickered as she pressed End on the cell phone.

Six

Charlotte was sitting on the front porch with Hannah, Buddy snoozing at her feet, when Lena and Amos came up the driveway. The familiar *clip-clop* of the horse hooves comforted her, but her stomach was a little fluttery as she waited to see if Amos would be welcoming or not. *Please behave yourself, Buddy.* She'd helped Hannah pull in the clothes from the line, fold them, and put them away accordingly. That was one thing she didn't think would ever change. Wash day was Monday for everyone in the community, although she couldn't recall why.

"This is late for them to be getting home, isn't it?" Charlotte eyed the moon peeking from behind the clouds as darkness descended.

"*Ya.* Maybe they stopped to eat somewhere in town. I know they're eager to see you, but *Daed* has to eat on schedule or he gets shaky." Hannah grinned. "And cranky."

Charlotte was still unsure how eager Amos would be to see her. But she and Hannah had made a meal out of buttered bread, and that was perfectly okay with Charlotte. She was sure she'd never get enough of it.

Amos tended to the horse and buggy while Lena hurried across the yard, stretching her arms out as she got closer. Charlotte ran down the steps and into the comfort of Lena's embrace.

"Sweet *maedel*, it's so *gut* to see you." Lena kissed her on the forehead, then eased away and cupped Charlotte's cheek. "We couldn't be happier that you've chosen to move here."

Charlotte glanced at Hannah, then back at Lena. "I'm so sorry I couldn't convince Jacob to come home."

Lena's eyes watered, but she raised her chin and said, "He just needs some time." She leaned down and gave Buddy a quick pat on the head. "And we are happy to have your dog too." She excused herself to go inside, and Hannah followed her with Buddy on her heels—thankfully. Buddy was sure to go nuts around Hannah's father when they met.

Charlotte waited on the porch for Amos. She considered meeting him with a hug but decided to follow the man's lead as he came up the porch steps. He stopped in front of her. "Jacob is okay?"

Charlotte corralled her disappointment at Amos's

lack of a welcome, keeping in mind they were all worried about Jacob. "Yes, he's fine. I'm sure he'll come to his senses soon." She paused. "But I'm happy to be here." It was a dumb thing to say. They all would have preferred Jacob over Charlotte.

Amos nodded as he reached for the handle on the screen door, his dark hair and beard speckled with more gray than she remembered. He had one foot over the threshold when Charlotte called out to him. He stopped but didn't turn around, as if waiting for her to add some brief comment so he could continue into the house.

"I'm sorry. I'm so sorry for everything. For all the lies the last time I was here." She'd asked herself for months why it was so important that Amos forgive her. It was their way to do so, but her need for Amos's approval bypassed any Amish ways. She loved him, and she wanted him to love her back. Despite her recent life hiccups, deep down she believed that God the Father was still with her, but she longed to be Amos's daughter during her time on earth.

He slowly stepped inside the house, closing the door behind him.

A tear slipped down Charlotte's cheek as she listened for Buddy to start barking, which was only going to make things worse. But all was quiet.

Daniel waited in his bedroom for Annie to get out of the upstairs bathroom. He'd already gone downstairs to see about using his parents' bathroom, but his mother occupied it. Was this how it was going to be with two pregnant women in the house? Did pregnant women have to go a lot, or was it just a coincidence that this was the third time this had happened today?

He headed down the hallway when he heard the pipes rumble, a familiar sound that meant the toilet had just been flushed. He met Annie in the hallway.

"You okay?"

"*Nee*. I'm never going to be okay. And I hate Jacob King." She scurried past him with her chin in the air, slamming her bedroom door. He was exhausted with worry about his mother and Annie. But as he lay down, he thought about the way Annie spat her feelings about Jacob, and he feared harboring such hatred might cause her to start slipping from her faith. Over the years, Daniel had been more like a father to Annie. He forced himself to stand up, yawned, and headed to Annie's room, trying to recall what it was like to be seventeen. He tapped on the door. He could see light underneath the door. He knocked again.

"Come in."

Daniel sat down in the rocking chair where his father had sat earlier in the day. "You can dislike Jacob for what he's doing, but you can't *hate* him, Annie." Although he could understand her strong emotions.

"I can and I do." She crossed one leg over the other beneath her blue dress. Daniel was surprised she hadn't bathed or gotten ready for bed yet.

Daniel shrugged. "You're hurting yourself more than him." He stood up, knowing Annie was in a mood he wasn't going to be able to change. He walked to the door, glancing over his shoulder. "You need to get ready for bed."

"I'll get ready when I feel like it."

He turned around. "You sound like a five-year-old."

She shrugged, and Daniel shook his head and went back to his own room. He'd heard the stories from others, how hormones get all out of whack when a woman is pregnant. *And I'm living with two of them.*

Tuesday morning, Jacob opened his eyes, confused for a moment. He lifted himself from the blanket on the living room floor. Standing barefoot in his boxers, his arms dangling at his sides, he stared at Charlotte's couch. At the stain—and at the letter he'd found in between the cushions of the couch. From her landlord. Charlotte wasn't moving voluntarily.

Annie had never betrayed his trust until last night. Why in the world did he listen to his ex-fiancée tell him to put bacon grease on a stain? He'd gotten out of that relationship because he felt called to do so. *This is how she treats me for following my calling?*

Jacob went to the kitchen, yawning. He found his mobile phone and tried to call Annie. She didn't answer until his seventh attempt.

"*Wie bischt*, Jacob."

He took a deep breath. "*Wie bischt*, Annie. I bet you are feeling smug right now."

"Whatever do you mean?"

Jacob almost grinned at her playful comment, despite the situation. "Charlotte's couch is ruined. But I guess you already know that, *ya*?"

She didn't say anything, and he was tempted to hang up, but something unexpected had happened since he'd been gone. He was starting to miss Annie. A lot. Still, he didn't want to go home, and he was pretty mad at her. But in an effort to keep his options open, he changed the subject. "I found a letter in between the couch cushions yesterday. Charlotte got thrown out of her apartment. I reckon that's why she had to move so fast."

Annie grunted. "And this surprises you? Charlotte—or shall I say Mary Troyer—has lied before."

"She didn't exactly lie. She said she was moving to somewhere less expensive."

"Well, she got her wish. She moved in with the Kings, which is free. Who knows what tales she will tell them while she's taking advantage of their hospitality."

Jacob rubbed the stubble on his chin. "Annie, it ain't like you to be so hostile. You sick or something?"

"*Ya*, I guess you could say I'm sick. I'm sick of the way

you have treated me. You are not the man I thought you were." Any hint of a playful tone was gone and replaced by a voice Jacob didn't recognize. "You've destroyed our lives, yet you think you can just call me at will to help with your problems."

Jacob scratched his chin, thinking she should be apologizing about the couch. He opened his mouth to tell her that he was sorry anyway and that he missed her, but she started screaming before he could utter a sound.

"I don't want anything to do with you. Don't call me again."

"You don't mean that." Jacob waited, but it was quiet. "Annie?"

She'd hung up on him again. In the back of his mind, he supposed he could try out this new life, and if it didn't work out, he could always go back to Annie. If going back to Annie wasn't a possibility—that made him want to go home more than ever. *I'm a mess.*

He flopped down on the couch like the pitiful, lost soul he was. Life had never seemed so confusing. He scooted to the far end of the couch, as far away as he could from the smelly brown stain. Maybe he should go home and see if he could work things out with Annie. Or at least talk to her, see if she might want to give the *Englisch* world a try with him. His stomach churned as he considered the possibility that Annie might not take him back. And time was running out before Jacob had to go to a hotel or go home.

Daniel was repairing the barn door when a buggy turned into the driveway. He hammered in the nail in his hand, put the two that were between his teeth in his pocket, then walked toward the visitors. It was Hannah and an *Englisch* woman.

"*Wie bischt.*" Hannah stepped out of the buggy and started walking across the yard toward Daniel. She nodded toward the other woman. "Do you remember our *gut* friend Charlotte?"

Daniel's stomach flipped. The woman who had pretended she was Mary Troyer looked much different in her *Englisch* clothes and with makeup on. But no matter how pretty she was, he didn't trust her, so he kept his eyes on Hannah.

"*Ya*, I remember her. I just didn't recognize her in *Englisch* clothes."

Charlotte took a step forward and spoke directly to him. "Um . . . I'm really sorry about that, about the lies, and—"

"*Nee, nee*," Hannah interrupted, waving a hand in the air. "That is all water under the bridge, and I'm sure Daniel understands why you did what you did, and—"

"No, Hannah." Charlotte kept her eyes on Daniel and took another step closer, until he was forced to look at her. "I need to tell those I lied to that I'm sorry.

Daniel, there really isn't an excuse for what I did. I was desperate to find out why my brother killed himself, but I should have never pretended to be Amish. It was wrong."

Daniel wasn't sure why she felt the need to apologize to him. He'd only been around the woman a handful of times and didn't even really know her.

"How is Jacob?" Daniel had trouble saying the lad's name.

Charlotte stuffed her hands in the pockets of her jeans. "He's okay, I guess. I'm hoping that some time to himself will help him get his thoughts straight. You remember what it was like to be seventeen, huh?"

Daniel felt his jaw tense. "*Ya*, I do. And Annie is seventeen. She isn't taking this *gut* at all."

Hannah touched Daniel on the arm, drawing his glare away from Charlotte.

"I think Jacob will come around. I really do," Hannah said as Charlotte stood next to her. "He has to decide soon. Tomorrow is the end of the month, when Charlotte's lease is up on her apartment. Jacob will have to go to a motel or come home. He told me on the phone that he didn't have a job or a place to live yet."

Daniel's jaw tensed again. The *Englisch* woman wasn't being totally truthful with Hannah and her family again. Annie had already told Daniel that Charlotte had been thrown out of her apartment. He considered saying so, but Hannah and her family were upset about Jacob.

Maybe this wasn't the right time. He snuck a glance in Charlotte's direction but turned back to Hannah.

"We just wanted to come pay a visit to your mother and Annie, to let them know that our thoughts and prayers are with them," Hannah said. "We wanted to come by sooner, but we had to have someone return the rental truck Charlotte used to get here. And Isaac brought two men who work at their furniture store to help store Charlotte's things in our basement." Hannah shook her head. "*Mei mamm* is very upset, too, but we have to trust that Jacob will realize he belongs here."

Daniel looked at Charlotte again and wondered if she was staying indefinitely, if she'd be moving into her brother's house. Or would she accept the Kings' hospitality until she got on her feet, then go back to where she came from?

The two women exchanged glances before Hannah said, "We're so happy Charlotte is here. She's gone through a bad breakup with her boyfriend, so we all need each other right now."

Daniel wasn't sure if Charlotte would receive a warm welcome from Annie. It was chaos with the women in his family anyway. Both of them throwing up, Annie trying to hide it from *Mamm*, and their mother not wanting anyone to know how sick she was, spending much of her time hiding in her bathroom. Daniel feared he might have to resume use of the old outhouse soon.

"Now isn't really a *gut* time, Hannah." Daniel

avoided her eyes, but when he finally caught her gaze, she frowned.

Daniel looked over his shoulder when the front door opened and his mother stepped over the threshold.

"Hannah!" *Mamm* waved, started down the steps, and met them in the yard. She immediately reached out for Charlotte's hand. "Hello, Charlotte. Thank you so much for taking care of Jacob in Houston. We're hoping he will get his head clear and come home soon. Annie is so upset."

Taking care of him? She made it easy for him to stay. Daniel shook his head without thinking, knowing he was scowling. He probably needed to go inside and warn Annie that Charlotte was here and tell her to behave herself. *Mamm* was bound to bring Charlotte and Hannah inside.

Hannah cleared her throat. "Um . . . Daniel said this isn't a *gut* time. We can come back if—"

"It's a perfectly *gut* time." *Mamm* motioned toward the house, apparently feeling better today. "Annie made an apple cobbler early this morning, so come in, come in."

Daniel moved quickly ahead of the women, then darted upstairs to find Annie. No surprise, she was in the bathroom. He tapped lightly on the door. "Annie, I'm just giving you a warning," he whispered. "Hannah King is downstairs, and she has Charlotte with her. You can say you're not feeling well if you want to, but *Mamm* is probably going to call you downstairs any minute."

Annie opened the door, her eyes wide. "What is she doing here?"

"Just visiting . . . she says." Daniel edged past his sister and into the bathroom while he had the chance.

~

Annie stood in the hallway, and just the sound of Charlotte's voice made her seethe. The *Englisch* woman wasn't a truthful person, but Annie also wondered how much influence Charlotte had on Jacob.

Sure enough, only moments later, *Mamm* yelled up for Annie to come downstairs. Annie opened her mouth to say she wasn't feeling well but instead closed it and marched down the stairs.

Her heart pounded, and she hesitated on the last step but then pushed forward with a smile plastered on her face. "*Wie bischt*, Hannah and Charlotte."

Annie had a hard time taking her eyes off Charlotte, who was dressed in blue jeans and a pink sweater. Her long dark hair fell almost to her waist, and she had on just enough makeup so that she looked naturally beautiful. But looks were deceiving, and Annie had been taught her entire life to avoid anything that enhanced a person's outer appearance, that beauty comes from within.

After both women returned the greeting, Annie walked to Hannah and hugged her. "*Danki* for coming. I know how upset you all are about Jacob, just like I am." She cut her eyes at Charlotte but quickly looked away.

"We just wanted to come check on you." Hannah eased out of the hug and nodded toward *Mamm*. "And we wanted to see how your *mamm* was feeling."

"*Ach*, well . . . it's been a long time since I've had morning sickness, but I will get through it." *Mamm* folded her hands together in front of her. "The good Lord will take care of me and this new baby coming into our lives."

Annie touched her stomach and thought about another life coming into their lives.

Mamm excused herself to the kitchen to get cobbler and coffee for Hannah and Charlotte, who both sat down on the couch. Annie sat down in the rocker facing them. "So, Charlotte . . ." She tried to keep her voice steady. "Jacob told me that you and your boyfriend broke up. What happened?"

Annie knew her voice didn't have an ounce of sympathy, and she didn't care.

"Um . . . he, uh . . . broke up with me." Charlotte sighed. "It just didn't work out."

"Why?" Annie sat taller, raising an eyebrow, but Hannah cleared her throat.

"So, have you talked to Jacob?"

Annie's cheeks dimpled. "*Ya*, I've talked to him."

"That's *gut*," Hannah said. "Is he thinking of coming home? Is he missing you?"

Annie glanced at Charlotte, then met Hannah's eyes. "*Ya*, he says he misses me, but it's hard to know what Jacob will do these days."

"I really do think he'll come around and be back home soon," Charlotte said.

Annie glowered but forced a quick recovery. "Charlotte, do you think you and your boyfriend will get back together, or is this a permanent move?"

Charlotte shifted her weight on the couch as she fidgeted with the hem of her sweater. "I, uh . . . he, well—"

Hannah cleared her throat. "Charlotte is here with us, taking time to heal as she gets settled into her new life. We're her family, so she is where she needs to be."

Charlotte's lips curved upward for a moment, but then her eyes watered a little.

"I started to think that Ryan—my boyfriend—might be cheating on me. I didn't have solid proof, just a gut feeling. I checked his phone. I was only going to do it once, but there were some suspicious text messages between him and a woman named Shelley. Checking his phone became a habit. He caught me looking one day and got upset. Things escalated, and he broke up with me."

You are a sneaky woman. Annie stored the thought with her distrust of Charlotte, who blinked her eyes a few times as she looked away, her cheeks flushed.

"But, as it turns out, my suspicions were right." Charlotte looked at Annie. "I saw him with Shelley right before I left to come here, and there was no doubt they were a couple, and had been for a while."

Annie brought a hand to her chest as her mother returned with a tray filled with glasses of tea. After everyone had a glass, *Mamm* went back to the kitchen and returned with cobbler. Annie half listened as her mother, Hannah, and Charlotte chatted about the baby *Mamm* was carrying, but she was still thinking about what Charlotte had said. Jacob would never cheat on her—Annie knew that for sure. Things were terrible between them right now, but Annie couldn't imagine that type of betrayal.

They all turned to the stairs when Daniel appeared on the landing. Annie thought he looked a bit pale. Probably concerned that she'd claw Charlotte's eyes out. But nothing was further from her mind.

Charlotte had never been so ready to leave.

"Well, that was weird," she said to Hannah as they got in the buggy. "It's clear that Daniel and Annie are not fond of me."

"*Nee, nee.* That's not it." Hannah clicked her tongue, instructing the horse to back up. "They're just upset about Jacob, like we are."

"I don't know. Eve was very nice, but the tension with Annie was thick. And Daniel would barely look at me. I think they remember Mary Troyer and all the lies I told."

"Charlotte, you've been forgiven. By God and by us. You must forgive yourself now."

Charlotte forced down the growing knot in her throat. Maybe she'd read Annie and Daniel wrong. Hannah was right about Charlotte needing to forgive herself. "I know," she said softly.

They rode in silence the rest of the trip. They'd already discussed where they were going next. And it wouldn't be an easy trip down memory lane for either of them.

Seven

Charlotte's eyes welled with tears when they pulled up to Ethan's house, and she avoided looking in the direction of the tree where Ethan had hanged himself. This had to be hard for Hannah, too, since she'd been engaged to Charlotte's brother before he died. But Hannah was very much in love with Isaac these days and couldn't wait to marry him in the fall. Still, the memories caused both women to sit quietly for a while.

"Isaac's done a great job fixing things up." Charlotte finally stepped out of the buggy, noticing the fresh coat of blue paint on the small house, along with a For Sale sign in the yard. "I still don't think Isaac charged me enough for the work he did."

"He didn't want to take any money at all from you," Hannah said as they walked up the porch steps, also repaired. "He finished everything about a month ago, and I don't think he's been back since."

Charlotte pulled the key from her purse and unlocked the door. The window in the living room had been repaired, and she could smell fresh paint. The interior walls were painted white, as Charlotte had requested, thinking it would help to make the small house look bigger.

She took a deep breath, then blew it out slowly as her eyes drifted around the room. Getting rid of the place felt so final. Charlotte thought about Jacob and wondered how he was doing. She suspected he would be heading home tomorrow, but as far as she knew, he hadn't committed to staying or leaving.

"Everything looks so different." Charlotte walked into the kitchen, also freshly painted. No furniture, no boxes. Just empty.

"The bed is still in the bedroom. Isaac knows a family who said they could use it, but they haven't picked it up yet."

Charlotte moved toward the bedroom, Hannah following her. They walked to the bed and eyed a brown spot on the mattress, as big as a football.

"Was this here before?" Charlotte cringed, thinking the house wouldn't show well with a dingy mattress inside. "It looks like someone spilled a soda or something."

"*Nee*, I never noticed a stain before. I removed the sheets when we were packing everything up. I would have remembered a spot like that."

"The door was locked. But we don't want kids coming in here to party. Let's make sure the back door is locked and check the windows." Charlotte walked to the only other exterior door in the house. "Locked." She and Hannah started checking the windows. Two were unlocked and big enough for someone to crawl through, so they secured them, then double-checked everything again.

Hannah eyed the bed. "I will let Isaac know about this. He has the key you gave him before you left. His friend might not want this bed anymore, but I'll ask Isaac to move it out of here either way."

Part of Charlotte wanted to keep the house since it was all that was left of Ethan. She'd even considered using it as a vacation getaway, but she couldn't stay in the house where Ethan had killed himself nearby, right out in the yard. Maybe she could have decorated the house in a way that wouldn't have constantly reminded her of her brother, but she'd still have to see the tree where he took his life, and that big oak would always haunt her. Plus, she needed the money from the house to help get her out of the financial mess she'd gotten herself into.

"Everything is locked up tight now. It was probably some kids hanging out." Charlotte locked the front door, and as they walked to Hannah's buggy, her eyes veered to the oak. "I hate that tree," she said to Hannah, noticing her friend was looking in the same direction.

"Me too," Hannah said softly.

~

Jacob woke up Thursday morning after a sleepless night. Later that morning, Charlotte's friends arrived to haul off the couch. When Jacob explained to the woman, Pam, what happened, she said Charlotte would probably just flip the cushion. *Why didn't I think of that?*

He packed his toiletries into his suitcase and took a final look around. He had to go home or find a hotel. Neither choice felt like the right one. But the thought that Annie might not take him back tugged him in the direction of home. And without a job, his money would be gone quickly if he stayed in a hotel. He picked up his cell phone and called Annie. She answered on the first ring.

"I know you said not to call, but I miss you." Jacob bit his bottom lip. *Guys don't cry.* Annie didn't say anything, but Jacob heard her breathing. "Did you hear me? I really miss you."

"*Ya*, I heard you."

Jacob sighed. "I love you, and I'm so sorry for the way I've been acting. I still want to be in the *Englisch* world, but one thing I've come to realize is, I'm never going to be happy without you in my life." He sat down on his suitcase and hung his head. "But I could never ask you to leave there. I know it's not what you want. So I'm having a conundrum."

"A what?"

"A problem." He'd learned that word in a book and liked the way it sounded rolling off his tongue, even if he'd rather not be having a conundrum. "But I know I love you, Annie."

She was quiet.

"You still there?" *Or did you hang up on me again?*

"I'm here."

"Do you still love me?" Jacob squeezed his eyes shut as his bottom lip trembled.

"I never stopped loving you, Jacob."

Annie closed her eyes tightly and pressed her lips together so she wouldn't blurt out what was heaviest on her heart, that she was carrying Jacob's child. No matter how sweet Jacob was trying to be, Annie worried that he would never be happy in Lancaster County. And she still wasn't sure that Jacob wouldn't be settling for something he didn't really want if he chose to come home. But her baby needed a father.

"Jacob . . ." She paused as a tear rolled down her cheek. "Don't . . . come back because of me."

"What are you saying?" His voice cracked. "You don't want to be with me anymore?"

She swiped at her eyes and took a deep breath. "I don't know. I don't understand how you just left me when we were planning to get married. And what if it happens again?"

"It won't happen again."

"Jacob, you discarded me, like I meant nothing to you. You were ready to give me up that easily. Marriage takes work and commitment. I—I don't trust you anymore."

They were quiet, but Annie thought she heard Jacob crying, which broke her heart. "I'm going to need some time to think about things. But what happens if you come back and get bored again, longing for a life outside of our district?"

"If I have to choose between having you or living here in Houston, I'm going to choose you."

"But that doesn't answer my question."

"I—I don't know. I'll make it work."

"I don't want you to *make it work*. I want you to be happy."

"Then come here. We can try living an *Englisch* life together. I never thought I'd ask you to do that, but I'm asking you."

Annie grimaced. "I can't. Even if I wanted to. My mother is pregnant, and at fifty-two, it's going to be a hard pregnancy. She said the doctor called it a high-risk pregnancy. I can't go anywhere right now."

Jacob was quiet.

"I can't tell you what to do, but I am telling you

not to come home because of me, because now I'm confused."

"If you need some time to think, I'll respect that. But please tell me you haven't given up on us for good."

Annie put a hand across her stomach. "Jacob, I'm just not sure how I feel."

~

Daniel packed everything into his toolbox Saturday morning, glad to have all the repairs on the barn done. He could check that off his list and move on to the broken slats on the back fence. He met Annie in the yard on the way.

"*Mamm* okay?" He dabbed at sweat on his forehead, glad the temperature was starting to warm up. Annie nodded, but Daniel could tell by the way her eyebrows were furrowed and her lips pressed together that something was on her mind.

"I think Jacob wants us to work things out."

Daniel still wasn't sure how he felt about Jacob, but he wanted Annie to be happy, and she needed a father for her child. "That's *gut*. That's what you want, right?"

"*Ya*, I thought I did. But how will I know that he won't do this again, get bored or feel smothered and leave again?"

"You can't be sure. You either choose to trust him or not." Daniel knew that was easier said than done. He feared it would still be awhile before he trusted another woman enough to open his heart to her. Edna had left a scar that on some days still felt like a raw wound.

"I love Jacob, but I'm not sure that's enough. What if he always longs for another type of life? He'll never be completely happy."

Daniel was glad to hear Annie working through her emotions like an adult. "These are choices only you can make. This is your journey, your path. But neither one of you gets to make choices based on just your own wants and needs anymore. There is a baby on the way."

"*Ya*. I know, and I'm going to pray about it."

Daniel nodded. "That's just what you should do. Let God show you the way."

She looked at the ground. "I did a bad thing."

Daniel stared at her. "What did you do?"

Annie told him the story about Charlotte's couch, and since he still hadn't decided how he felt about Charlotte, he couldn't help but laugh.

"It's not funny. Now she has a couch with a permanent stain on it to go along with her other problems."

Daniel watched his sister's expression take on an air of sympathy. "You've decided you like Charlotte now, since you both got dumped?" It was harsh, and Daniel wished he could take it back. He held up a hand when Annie opened her mouth. "I'm sorry. I shouldn't have said that. But don't forget, Charlotte isn't a truthful person."

"I know."

Daniel shook his head, grinning. "But bacon grease? I used to think Jacob was a smart young man, always schooling himself past what was required, but I'm not sure anyone could have talked me into pouring grease on a stain."

Annie frowned. "Jacob's not dumb. He's confused. Everyone gets confused sometimes."

"You realize that you do that all the time, don't you?"

"What?"

"You talk badly about him, then you defend him. You go back and forth." He pointed a finger at her. "But you'd better decide what you are going to do about this baby situation. You are going to have to tell *Mamm* and *Daed*. And Jacob."

"I don't want him to come back just because I'm with child."

Daniel motioned for her to walk with him toward the back fence that he planned to repair. "It sounds like he already wants to come back."

"What do you think I should do? What if I get shunned?"

Daniel thought for a moment. "If you got shunned, it would probably only be until you and Jacob got married and talked to the elders, explaining that you know what you did was wrong."

"But where would we go? We didn't think we'd have to find a place to live until we got married. And Jacob gave up his job too."

"I don't know, Annie. But these are things *Mamm* and *Daed* can help you to figure out. I'm not sure what to tell you."

They stopped at the fence. Annie pulled her sweater tighter around her. "I'm scared to tell them. I can already see the looks on their faces when I tell them what Jacob and I did. But I didn't think a girl could get pregnant by"—she looked away, blushing—"by doing it just one time. We agreed to never do it again, until we were married."

Daniel was glad to hear that part, but he shrugged. "I don't know. But you need to at least talk to *Mamm*. Maybe she'll be more sympathetic since she's pregnant too." He grinned. "And then once it's all out in the open, we need to post a bathroom schedule."

"Huh?" She shriveled up her face.

"Never mind. Just talk to them."

Annie was quiet, nervously twisting the string of her prayer covering. She finally unraveled her finger from the string. "Anyway, *Daed* is inside eating lunch. That's what I came out here to tell you, that lunch is ready."

"I'm going to finish the fence, then I'll be in. Maybe you should take advantage of this time and go talk to them."

Annie's feet were rooted to the ground, but she nodded. His sister slowly walked back to the house, leaving Daniel alone with his thoughts, which were all over the place.

He wasn't normally a mean guy. He recalled how rude he'd been to Charlotte and wondered if he'd treated her unfairly. Maybe he needed to rethink his opinion of Charlotte and not judge her when he might not have all the facts.

Fifteen minutes later, Daniel wondered how it was going inside the house, if Annie had chosen to tell their parents about the baby. He'd finished up and was about to go in when a buggy turned into the driveway. He dropped his hammer when he saw that it was Edna. Alone. It was a long trek to the front yard from where he was, but he recognized Edna's walk way before her face came into view. She had more of a glide than a walk. Daniel knew she wasn't here to see him, but it might not be a good time for her to go inside either.

"*Wie bischt*, Daniel," Edna said as she closed the distance between them.

Edna didn't look any older than Annie, even at twenty-four. She was a small woman, but her dimples added to her youthful appearance. He tipped his straw hat at her and fought to calm the butterflies in his stomach, hoping there would come a day when he wouldn't feel this way around her.

"Can we go somewhere to talk privately?" She looked around. "Maybe in the barn?"

"Okay. Is everything all right?" Daniel got in step with her as they crossed the yard.

She shook her head. "*Nee*, not really."

Daniel closed the barn door behind them. "Are you sick? Is John sick? What's wrong?"

Edna looked down and bit the edge of her bottom lip. "Marrying John was a mistake." She walked until she was inches from his face. It was impossible for Daniel not to think about all the kisses they'd shared in this barn, long before she'd married John. He couldn't breathe. He couldn't move. She lifted up on her toes, and Daniel instinctively leaned his lips down to hers. She cupped his cheeks and pulled him closer, kissing him the way a married woman should not kiss another man. He grabbed her shoulders and eased her away.

"What are you doing? You're married." He shook his head and kicked at the dirt floor. "I shouldn't have let that happen."

Edna touched his cheek. "It's you I want, Daniel. If I can't have you full-time, then can't we at least be together some of the time?"

Daniel clenched his teeth. "*Nee*, we can't." He valued marriage, and no matter how he'd once felt about Edna, or how tempted he might be, he was not going to commit adultery. Daniel had heard gossip awhile back that Charlotte's brother, Ethan, had been seeing Edna while she was dating John. He hadn't believed such a rumor. Until now.

She tried to kiss him again, but he grabbed her hands. "You need to go, Edna. Back to your husband."

"I know you still care about me . . . and want me."

He'd thought he did, but seeing her like this, seductive and married, made his stomach churn, and his heart hurt for John. "Go home."

Daniel turned his back to her and left the barn. Maybe now he'd have some luck getting her out of his heart for good.

Eight

Charlotte finished her breakfast Sunday morning, glad it was an "off" weekend for church. She'd attended church most Sundays back home, except for the past couple of weeks that followed her breakup with Ryan. He went to the same church, and she hadn't been ready to run into him there. She wondered if he was going now. Maybe he was attending the service with Shelley. She forced the thought away, unwilling to shed any more tears about Ryan.

But church at home was forty-five minutes, as opposed to the three-hour worship service in Amish country that was held every other week. She'd thought that she was doing all the right things in God's eyes, trying to be a better person, going to church, and praying every day. But when things fell apart with Ryan, she'd wondered if God was punishing her. But if Ryan was attending church, he needed to do some serious praying about his role in their demise.

She stifled a yawn as she helped Lena and Hannah clear the breakfast dishes, feeling good about the editing work she'd gotten done the past few days, mostly in the evenings. It was challenging to keep her phone and computer charged, but she had two portable power packs, so that helped. And her Mac Pro—a hand-me-down from Ryan when he'd purchased a new computer—held a charge for five to seven hours. But someone usually went to town for something, and Charlotte and her electronics tagged along. They'd hit a coffee shop or diner somewhere along their route and everyone would find a plug. Her Amish friends tried to be discreet about it, but Charlotte was pretty sure most of them had cell phones. The younger people anyway.

Hannah and her parents went to bed around eight. Charlotte needed to go to bed then, too, so she wasn't yawning all through breakfast like she had this morning. But it was a hard schedule to adapt to. She wanted to be helpful during the day, but she needed to make some headway with her projects, so she'd been staying up late to work.

She peeked into the living room where Buddy was sleeping on Amos's lap, which was surprising since Buddy had never liked any man, except for Ryan.

When her phone vibrated on the kitchen counter, she

went to answer it, surprised to see Jacob calling from the phone she'd given him.

"I want to come home," Jacob said when Charlotte answered. "I tried to call *mei mamm*, but I don't think she keeps her phone turned on. Is she nearby where I can talk to her?"

Charlotte held the phone to her chest and whispered to Hannah and Lena. "Jacob wants to come home." She brought the phone to her ear, but Lena was already right beside Charlotte, whispering that she wanted to talk to him. "I think that's great. Here's your mom."

Charlotte handed Lena the phone, then she helped Hannah clean the kitchen while Lena paced on the porch, phone to her ear.

Hannah handed Charlotte a dish to dry. "Praise God that Jacob is coming home. I wonder if he will marry Annie now."

Charlotte had no idea what was going on in Jacob's head. "I hope so."

"I can't imagine how it would be if Jacob had stayed in the *Englisch* world, especially if he'd stayed in Texas, so far away. But he's not baptized yet, so he has that choice." She rinsed another dish under the faucet and handed it to Charlotte. "But Annie is baptized. She has always been so strong in her faith and sure that she wanted to marry Jacob."

They both stayed quiet, lost in their own thoughts. Charlotte was wondering if any checks were on the way.

She'd received her first piece of forwarded mail the day before, but it was a bill. She was trying to decide what to do first when she got caught up on her bills—buy an inexpensive car or have Ethan's house wired for electricity—if it hadn't sold yet.

Lena came back inside, and when Charlotte saw her gleaming, she was hopeful that everything would be all right, at least for Jacob. Hannah hurried to her mother.

"Well, what did he say?" Hannah wiped her hands on her apron.

"He's been in a hotel, but he's going to get a train ticket home tomorrow. He's homesick. He misses Annie." Lena hugged Hannah and then pressed her palms together. "Charlotte, you were right. Jacob just needed some time to himself to see things clearly." Lena beamed. "The Lord has answered my prayers."

"Wonderful news." Charlotte leaned against the kitchen counter and breathed a sigh of relief.

Lena went into the living room to share the good news with her husband. Amos had said very little to Charlotte, mostly just answering when spoken to. Charlotte needed to know if he was ever going to forgive her. She'd mentioned it to both Lena and Hannah separately, and both women had said Amos forgave her a long time ago. But Charlotte wasn't convinced.

Lena walked back into the kitchen. "*Ach*, Charlotte ... there is one thing—" She tapped a finger to her chin. "Jacob said he needed to talk to you about your couch."

"What about it?" She brought a hand to her chest. "Did Pam and Phillip not pick it up?"

"Um . . . they did, but I think Jacob might have spilled something on one of the cushions."

"I'm sure it's fine." Charlotte loved that couch. It was her one big splurge two years ago, before she drifted into a world of credit card debt. "I can just flip the cushion." *Or get it cleaned and then see if Pam can sell it for me.*

Later that morning, Charlotte took advantage of some downtime and decided to take a walk and think. But it was a short walk as she realized she didn't want time to think. She seemed to do better when she stayed busy. But she did manage to think about her odd recollection of the woman and child at the convenience store. She'd been thinking about it less and less, and nothing about being in Amish country had triggered any additional memories, so maybe it was just something she'd literally dreamed up. She decided to push the thought from her mind. She had enough to deal with without creating more problems for herself.

She returned in time for lunch, but she opted to step outside to make some calls, reminders to those who owed her money. Her Amish friends wouldn't approve of her making work calls on a Sunday. She told the others to go ahead and eat without her. After she'd left another message for the client who continued to avoid her, she noticed someone had left her a voice mail. She'd deleted Ryan's contact information, but she recognized his voice right away. "Aunt Maureen called. She said she'd tried to reach you without success. She said to tell you that she wishes you well and hopes you'll find a good counselor there." There was a long pause. "I'm sorry about the way everything happened, Charlotte."

She considered hurling the phone out into the yard as Ryan's voice mail burrowed into her skin like a tick. That's what he was. He'd sucked the love right out of her, infected her with lies, and let go of her when someone better came along. Maybe he needed to get his own counseling and quit worrying about whether or not Charlotte continued therapy.

Lena opened the door and peeked out. "Are you going to eat?"

Charlotte turned around and shook her head. "No, but I'll help clean up. I'm still full from breakfast." It was partially true, although she hadn't turned down homemade bread—which was served at every meal—since she'd arrived.

"*Nee, nee.* Hannah and I can clean up. You enjoy this warmer weather." Lena grinned. "And you can sneak yourself some buttered bread later when you're hungry."

"You know I will," Charlotte said, careful not to let her voice crack.

She'd only been feeling sorry for herself about five

minutes when Amos came out of the house, holding his straw hat in his hands. She stood up from the porch step so he could get by her.

Amos put his hat on as he passed her on the steps, but when he hit the grass, he turned around and looked at her. Granted, they'd mostly only seen each other during mealtimes and nightly devotions, so maybe now Amos would tell her he was glad she was here, that he forgave her . . . something.

"It's a pretty day today," he said, the hint of a smile on his face.

Charlotte's lips curved upward as she brought a hand to her forehead to block the sun. "Yes, it is. It's starting to feel like spring."

He nodded, gave a quick wave, and said, "Enjoy your day," then walked out to the fields.

Annie paid the cabdriver, which took the last of her cash, then hurried up the sidewalk to her aunt's house. She'd left with only her purse and the clothes on her back. But after the way things had gone at home, she didn't have a choice. She knocked on Aunt Faye's door, glancing over her shoulder as the taxi disappeared in the darkness. She knocked again and thought about how dumb it was to show up here in the middle of the night. Annie hadn't seen her great-aunt since she was twelve. Aunt Faye and

Uncle James had left the Old Order five years ago and converted to Mennonite. Aunt Faye had chosen to rent out several bedrooms in her home after Uncle James died a couple of years later. At least that's what Annie had heard from her mother. Harrisburg was almost an hour away by car, but she suspected it hadn't been the distance that kept them from visiting or attending her uncle's funeral. Aunt Faye and Uncle James had been shunned. Maybe Aunt Faye would be more understanding about Annie's situation than her parents.

A woman wearing a pink robe opened the door, her eyes half open. "Can I help you? Who's knocking on my door at this hour?"

Annie almost didn't recognize her aunt. She had always been a tall woman, but Annie didn't remember her being so hunched over, and wrinkles connected like a spiderweb across her face. She was much thinner than Annie remembered also. But when her aunt flashed a set of pearly whites, Annie remembered why she'd liked her as a child. Aunt Faye's eyes seemed to get bigger when she smiled. It made her look a little like a cartoon character, especially since she had really big ears. Annie hadn't been allowed to watch television growing up, but there were a few times she'd seen cartoons when they'd visited *Englisch* friends.

"*Aenti* Faye?"

Annie's great-aunt opened her eyes even wider, still smiling. "Do I know you, child?"

"It's me. Annie. Eve and Lucas's daughter. I'm sorry to be showing up in the middle of the night, but . . ." Annie blinked her swollen eyes, having no idea what she'd do if Aunt Faye turned her away. And without realizing how fearful she'd become, she burst into tears again.

Faye pulled the screen open and pulled Annie into her arms. "Oh my. Oh my."

"I didn't know where else to go." Annie wept so hard she was gasping for breath. "I'm with child. *Mamm* and *Daed*—" Her voice broke before she could finish her sentence.

"You came to the right place," Aunt Faye whispered as she held her.

~

Daniel propped his elbows on the kitchen table and laid his forehead in his hands. He'd rarely heard his parents bicker, but today topped any past arguments. They were in their bedroom with the door shut, but his mother was screaming, and Daniel could hear every word. "You were much too hard on her, Lucas. What if she doesn't come back?"

"She has shamed us, her and that boy!"

Daniel cringed. He didn't think he'd ever heard his father so angry. Lucas Byler was usually content letting his wife handle family matters, but it was clear earlier today that he was the one in charge when he'd blasted Annie for being unwed and pregnant. At one point, Daniel had thought his father might strike Annie, something he'd never done. But instead, he whipped her with his words until Annie looked beaten, her face flushed and red, her eyes puffy. Worst of all was the way Annie had hunched over, cowering from *Daed*, one hand across her stomach, like she, too, feared he might hit her. It was awful to watch, and Daniel felt sick to his stomach. He recalled what his father had said earlier about a baby being a blessing, no matter what. That must not pertain to his unmarried, pregnant daughter.

Annie had left a note saying she was leaving, then snuck out the back door at some point during the night. Daniel had tried to call Annie several times, but she never answered. He'd even tried to call Jacob, thinking that maybe Annie had contacted him. Apparently Charlotte had gotten the boy a phone, and thankfully Annie had given Daniel his phone number. Everyone in his family was abusing their cell phone privileges; he suspected that was the case at Jacob's house too. To his knowledge, neither of his parents had let Jacob's family know that Annie was gone. Daniel was going to wait until tomorrow to notify them, in case Annie changed her mind and came home. His mother was yelling again, and Daniel didn't think that could be good in her condition. But he sat quietly at the table and prayed for peace for all of them.

~

Charlotte watched Jacob step out of the cab and walk across the yard Tuesday afternoon, toting the same boxy suitcase. The prodigal son was home. *Thank You, God.* She waited until Lena and Hannah quit hugging Jacob, then she gave him a quick embrace and stepped aside so Amos could greet his son. If they'd been angry with him for leaving, they'd tucked those emotions away and chosen joy at his return. Charlotte was glad he was wearing a long-sleeved shirt, but someone was eventually going to see his tattoo. Charlotte hoped she wasn't around on that day.

It was thirty minutes later when someone knocked on the door. Hannah let Daniel in as Buddy jumped from Amos's lap and scurried toward Annie's brother. Daniel skidded to a halt in the middle of the room, barely noticing the barking dog at his feet.

"Jacob, what are you doing here?" Daniel walked toward Jacob, who was sitting in the rocking chair eating a slice of apple pie.

"He called on Sunday and told us he was coming home. He wanted to surprise Annie, with high hopes they can work things out." Lena brought her hands to her chest, smiling. "He left by train Sunday and just got home a little while ago. Isn't that wonderful?"

Daniel took off his straw hat and held his palm to

his forehead as he glared at Jacob. "Have you talked to Annie? Do you know where she is?"

Everyone got quiet, waiting for Daniel to go on. When he didn't, Lena said, "Daniel, what are you talking about?"

Amos was sitting on the couch reading the newspaper. He took off his reading glasses and folded the paper, searching Daniel's face like the rest of them. Charlotte scooped Buddy up and stroked his head until he finally stopped barking.

"Annie's gone. She left a note saying she was leaving." Daniel glared at Jacob. "I'd hoped she'd change her mind and be back home by now, but since she's not, I thought I better let everyone know."

Charlotte looked around at the expression of shock registering on everyone's face.

"We don't know where she is. We've called around . . . no one knows. Has she tried to call any of you?" Daniel glanced at the Kings, then glared at Jacob again.

Jacob choked down the pie he'd been holding in his mouth, his eyes round. "Uh, my phone isn't charged."

Daniel hung his head, shaking it.

"Why did she run away?" Jacob's voice rose an octave.

Daniel clenched his fists at his sides.

"I'm so confused," Charlotte whispered.

"Why did she run away?" Jacob asked again, more emphatically.

Daniel's face turned bright red as he walked toward

Jacob. He reached down and grabbed the collar of Jacob's blue shirt. Lena gasped and Amos stood from his spot on the couch.

"Annie is pregnant. Pregnant and alone. You have dishonored everyone, especially Annie."

Charlotte couldn't breathe. "Um . . ." She couldn't seem to gather her thoughts. "I thought Eve was pregnant."

Daniel looked over his shoulder at Charlotte, then he finally let go of Jacob and turned to face the rest of the family. "*Mamm* is pregnant too."

Charlotte narrowed her eyebrows. "And no one knows where Annie is?"

Daniel shook his head. "*Nee*. Annie should have known better than to upset *Mamm* this way while she's pregnant, but we're still very worried about Annie." He glowered at Jacob as he leaned his weight forward.

"Annie is pregnant?" Lena fell onto the couch, her eyes tearing up as she frowned at her son. Amos had his arms crossed, his expression dark. Charlotte glanced at Hannah, who hadn't said a word. Her friend stared at Jacob, looking sick.

"I've been trying to call Annie. She and my parents had a big fight. She told them she was with child, and *mei daed* went *ab im kopp*, yelling at her." Daniel turned to Jacob, his fists balled at his sides again, his jaw tensing.

"Annie's pregnant." Jacob spoke softly, as if to himself, then turned as white as the walls.

Charlotte stared at the faces around the room. She'd

run from her troubles back home, but there seemed to be even more drama here.

Daniel scrambled to pull his phone out of his pants pocket when it started to ring. He listened for a few moments, the muscles in his face relaxing, then he hung up. "Annie is okay. That was *Mamm*, and she said that Annie showed up at our great-aunt's house in Harrisburg. *Aenti* Faye said Annie doesn't want to talk to anyone."

Jacob stood up slowly and faced Daniel, stretching taller, but Jacob still wasn't as tall as Annie's brother. "I will go bring her home safely."

"*Nee*. You will not go near her right now. I will hire a driver to take me to Harrisburg in the morning." Daniel's nostrils flared. He was a nice-looking guy, but right now he looked a bit scary.

"I'll drive you," Charlotte interjected, hoping to help. "Oops. Never mind. I forgot, I don't have a car."

"I heard today that our regular driver is down with shingles. She's not making trips anywhere right now," Lena said, sniffling and clutching a tissue.

Amos cleared his throat. Everyone got quiet as he walked across the room to the coatrack by the door. Next to it was a hook with several key rings hanging on it. He picked the one with a single key, then walked to Charlotte and held it out to her. "There is a Ford automobile in the old barn at the very back of the property." He cut his eyes at Lena, whose face had fallen into a frown, then he turned back to Charlotte. "I was going to give it to you to use until you could get your own car, but it needs a battery." He shrugged. "There's a new battery in the barn. I just hadn't gotten around to . . . uh . . . telling Lena the automobile was still on the property." He cleared his throat again. "I will put a battery in it early tomorrow morning so you can drive Daniel to see about Annie."

Lena stood up and put her hands on her hips. "It's a long walk to that old barn. I bet I haven't been out there in two years. I thought you'd gotten rid of that thing after you took it on trade for the money Albert Hines owed you."

Amos shook his head before he said quietly, "*Nee, nee.* It's just been sitting out there."

"If the bishop knew . . ." Lena huffed out a long breath.

"It ain't like I'm driving it around town." Amos held out his hands to Buddy, who lapped at them before he practically dove into Amos's arms. *Unbelievable.* "Hope you can drive a stick shift," he said as he and Buddy walked back to his seat on the couch.

"Uh, yes, I can." Charlotte resisted the urge to cry, touched that Amos would want to help her. But once she let the thought settle in her mind, she knew this was more about Annie and getting to her as quickly as possible. She looked at the key and then at Daniel. She waited for him to refuse Amos's offer, but Daniel nodded and made his way to the door.

It's gonna be a long ride to Harrisburg tomorrow.

Nine

Jacob sat at the kitchen table with his parents after Daniel was gone. *Daed* asked Charlotte and Hannah to go upstairs. After they had left the room, his father put his palms flat on the table as his mother fidgeted. Jacob thought about being a father, how he'd left Annie, how Annie's parents had yelled at her until she felt she had to run away. There wasn't much his father could say to him right now that would make him feel any worse than he already did.

"When Annie comes home, you will marry her." Amos King didn't speak often, so when he did, his authoritative tone demanded respect. Jacob nodded, finding himself back where he was before any of this started—feeling trapped. But what choice did he have? He was going to be a father, he loved Annie, and he planned to do the right thing. Once again, he recalled Charlotte's words: *The grass isn't always greener on the other side.* But he hadn't really given the *Englisch* life much of a chance. His desire to return to Annie had been stronger than his need to have freedom. But once his father stole his freedom, it was all he could think about again.

They all sat quietly. Jacob waited for someone to yell at him, but his mother just wept quietly. Then both of his parents stood up, went to their bedroom, and closed the door. Their disappointment in Jacob hung in the air like the Houston pollution he'd wallowed around in until a couple of days ago.

Charlotte shuffled straight to the coffee percolating on the stove the next morning. Something was baking in the oven, but it wasn't bread. Sniffing the air, she recognized Lena's homemade cinnamon rolls cooking. She eased the oven open and breathed in the heavenly aroma. Movement out the kitchen window caught her attention.

No way. She took a few steps closer and gawked out the window until footsteps came up behind her.

Lena chuckled. "Not what you were expecting, *ya*?"

Charlotte stared at Amos and Daniel putting

a battery in the vehicle she was supposed to drive to Harrisburg. "It's a truck," she said with a hitch in her voice, mixed with a healthy dose of fear. "It's old. Very old." She pursed her lips. *And red. Very, very red. And dirty.*

Lena huffed as she cozied up beside Charlotte. "Amos doesn't fool me for one minute. That's a '57 Chevy, and even Amish men seem smitten with automobiles, especially those the *Englisch* consider classics, like that one."

Charlotte brought a hand to her chest. "I wonder if it's been driven since 1957." She eyed the big dent on the left rear bumper, and it looked like it tilted to one side.

Lena put a hand on Charlotte's back. "We will pray for safe travels for you and Daniel."

Charlotte thought about the U-Haul she'd driven across the county. *I can do this.* But she nodded and whispered, "Yes, prayers please."

Daniel stood next to Charlotte, along with Lena and Amos, all of them staring at the vehicle that Charlotte was to drive with Daniel to Harrisburg. Isaac had picked up Hannah a few minutes ago. They had plans to spend the day together, and everyone had insisted Hannah keep those plans. There wasn't anything Hannah could do for Annie right now. Jacob was still asleep, weary from his travels, Daniel presumed.

"It's not much of a looker." Amos ran a hand the length of his beard. "But it will get the job done. Our prayers are with you, that all goes well with Annie."

Daniel appreciated those prayers, but as he eyed the lopsided truck with more than just age in its disfavor, he quietly asked the Lord to guide their way today. He opened the driver's side door for Charlotte, giving it a final jerk when it seemed to stick midway. She climbed inside and Daniel went to the other side. Same problem with the passenger door. Inside, the musty smell mingled with something that resembled mold. Or maybe a dead animal. Exposed springs protruded from the seat in between them, and most of the dashboard was hanging loose, although Amos had assured them that the gauges worked. But the vehicle started right up when Charlotte turned the key—although she stalled it four times trying to get out of the driveway. She needed to get familiar with that clutch.

"Are you sure you know what you're doing?" He tried to keep the impatience from his voice since Charlotte was doing them a favor by making the trip.

Charlotte's knuckles were white as she clutched the oversized steering wheel. She briefly turned his way. "Of course I don't know what I'm doing." The truck jerked and died again when she pushed the long gear stick to the right.

"Maybe I should drive," he mumbled under his breath as she turned the key to restart the engine.

Scowling, she faced him again. "Do you know how to drive?"

"*Nee*, not really. But maybe better than you." He grinned.

She didn't say anything for a while as they bounced down the gravel driveway. It seemed to take all of Charlotte's might to turn the steering wheel onto the road. Daniel wondered how she'd do on the highway.

"No power steering," she said, grumbling.

With the windows down, Charlotte's long brown hair blew in the wind. She wasn't wearing any makeup this morning, which Daniel thought was a much better look for her. With that thought, he was reminded of her time disguised as Mary Troyer. Daniel never condoned lying, but maybe he'd reacted too harshly to Charlotte's deception. She must have loved her brother very much to go to the lengths she did to find out what pushed him to end his life.

"I hate to ask you this . . ." She grunted as she pushed the long stick shift forward. "But in all the commotion, I didn't know I had a voice mail message. Ethan's house is listed with a real estate agent, and she left a message saying that she had a showing for the house yesterday. When they got there, water was running out the front door." She rolled her eyes. "Obviously that showing didn't go well, and she turned the water off inside, but she said it's a mess." She glanced at Daniel, a strained look on her face. "We have to go right by there. Do you mind if we take five minutes to stop and see how much damage there is?"

"That is fine." A few minutes wasn't going to make a difference in Annie's mood, one way or the other, once they arrived in Harrisburg.

"Thanks." She kept taking her hands off the wheel to push back wild strands of hair that were flying all over the place. It was warm enough to have the windows rolled down, but with each bump dust swirled around them and found its way inside the truck. Daniel could almost taste it. She successfully parked the truck in front of Ethan's house and forced the door open, reaching into her purse for a key. "I'll be right back."

Something didn't seem right about letting her go inside by herself, so Daniel followed her up the porch steps. She unlocked the door and walked inside.

"This can't be happening," she said in a voice that sounded like she was on the verge of tears.

Daniel sidled up to her, both of them standing on the wet floor.

"Isaac did so much work on this house so I can sell it." Charlotte looked up at Daniel with teary eyes. "I guess a pipe broke."

Daniel went to the kitchen and pulled open the cabinet doors beneath the sink. It was dry, so he walked to the bathroom and went through the same process.

"The pipe isn't broken under here, but some fittings have come loose and it's separated," he said when he heard footsteps slow behind where he was squatting on the floor.

"Please tell me this is an easy fix, something I can do." Charlotte knelt on the floor beside him and peered over his shoulder.

"*Ya*, it is." He briefly explained the process to her. "It shouldn't take Isaac too long to make the repairs."

"No, I'm not asking him. Isaac is a good man, and he has gone way above the call of duty to help me with this house. I'll do it. Surely I can find some instructions online or something. Do you think the parts are expensive?"

Daniel appreciated her willingness to make the repairs on her own, but if she was going to have to go onto a computer for directions about a simple plumbing repair, she might just make things worse if she didn't do it correctly. He stood up, but she was still studying the problem.

"I will repair your plumbing after we get Annie home."

Charlotte got to her feet and gazed up at him with such admiration, it almost made him feel sorry for her. She blinked her eyes a few times. "You would do that?"

"*Ya*. The least I can do since you are risking your life to drive that truck all the way to Harrisburg." He grinned, hoping she would too. Daniel wasn't sure he could deal with any more crying women. There would probably be enough of that when they got to Aunt Faye's house.

Charlotte smiled as they made their way across the damp floors, but she paused at the entrance to the bedroom. "Someone left this dingy mattress. Isaac said he'd haul it off." She sighed. "He's such a good man."

Daniel agreed. As he glanced around, he knew the wood floors were at risk of buckling if they didn't get them dry soon, but he'd work on drying the floors when he tackled the broken pipe later. It sounded like Isaac had spent a lot of time helping Charlotte, but he could lend a hand as payment for the ride. Right now, he was feeling anxious about getting Annie, and equally as nervous about the ride there.

Charlotte breathed deeply and took one last walk around, then she bowed her head and prayed for the person who would end up living in this house, that it would be a place of great happiness and peace for them.

Daniel followed her to the front door, she locked up, and they headed down the porch steps. She tried to avoid looking at the tree she hated, but her eyes inevitably drifted in that direction. She quickened her steps to the truck. The antique started on the first try, and she muscled it into gear. When she searched for the rearview mirror to have another look at Ethan's house, she saw that there actually wasn't one. Luckily the truck had side mirrors. They bounced all over the place until they eventually made their way to Lincoln Highway. As they picked up speed, she turned to Daniel. "Can you hold the steering wheel?"

"Uh, *ya* . . . okay." He reached across the seat and took hold of it while Charlotte wrangled her hair into a ponytail with a twisty she kept on her wrist for such a purpose.

"Thanks." She took possession of the wheel again. "This trip is going to be challenging enough without my hair blocking my view."

Daniel stayed quiet. Surely he was worried about Annie. Even Charlotte's heart hurt for Annie. To be seventeen and pregnant in Charlotte's world would be scary, so she knew Annie must bc terrified.

"Charlotte, the more I think about it, I'm worried that if we let your floors stay wet like that, they might buckle. Maybe we need to pick up some towels and go back, at least mop up the extra water that flowed from the bathroom across the living room."

She briefly looked at him but switched her eyes back to the road. "They've probably been wet for a while. It's just a house. This is Annie's life, her future. The house can wait."

~

Daniel allowed himself a long look at Charlotte since she was focused on the cars in front of them. He wanted to dislike her. If he didn't like her, then he wouldn't be attracted to her. And for Daniel, attraction ran deep, but that desire needed to be matched internally as well. Charlotte might turn heads for her outer beauty, but if she wasn't pretty on the inside, then it wasn't real. But every time he was sure they wouldn't ever be friends, she surprised him by doing or saying something nice. Again, he wondered if he had prejudged her unfairly.

They were quiet for a while, and Daniel tried not to cringe every time they jerked and swayed when Charlotte shifted gears or sped up or slowed down. He glanced at the seat between them. He'd already noticed springs protruding from the seat where her huge black purse now sat. He noticed a book sticking out the top, one side of the binding poking out. The silence was becoming awkward. "What are you reading?" he asked her.

She blushed. "Uh . . . it's . . . I guess what you'd call a self-help book."

"What do you need help with?" It was none of his business, but he figured conversation would make the trip go quicker.

"I broke up with my boyfriend." She cleared her throat. "Actually, he broke up with me."

Daniel knew this, but he nodded. "Did you lie to him?" It was an awful thing to say, and he wished he could take it back when he saw her lip tremble slightly.

"I'm sorry," he said before she could respond. "I shouldn't have said that."

"No, it's okay. I'm sure most of the people in your district think I'm a liar." She glared at him, tears in her eyes. "But Lena, Jacob, and Hannah have forgiven me, so you can think whatever you want."

Daniel noticed she didn't include Amos, but it was probably an oversight.

"I'm sorry," he said again. "I know you were trying to find out what happened to your *bruder*."

Daniel couldn't imagine how a book could help heal a broken heart. Only time and God took care of such things.

~

Charlotte was tempted to tell Daniel that he was a jerk, but he'd offered to make repairs at Ethan's house, so she bit her tongue and decided to offer up information that Daniel may or may not know. "Ethan suffered from depression. It's as much a disease as cancer or anything else that can be terminal. I guess no one in your community recognized it as such." She glanced his way. "I'm not blaming anyone. It's just that if Ethan had gotten some counseling, maybe things would have turned out differently." She shrugged. "I don't know." She signaled to change lanes, although there was no indication on the dash that the signal lights even worked. She was going to be sore after manhandling this steering wheel for the hour drive there, then back again. She couldn't imagine driving this every day. "Ethan and I had a rough childhood," she added.

She'd grown weary of Dr. Levin's insistence that Charlotte needed to face the demons in her life, her parents. Charlotte didn't even remember the last time she'd seen either of her parents. Maybe ten years ago. Hopefully, one day it would all become so fuzzy that she wouldn't remember her parents at all—or her time in foster care.

She stared ahead and counted backward from one hundred, something she'd always done to push certain memories to the back of her mind, to make room for something more pleasant. Her money woes weren't exactly pleasant, but they were certainly better than thoughts about her childhood. And with each day, she thought less and less about Ryan.

"Do you have those thoughts?" Daniel spoke the words softly, like he was afraid to ask. "I mean, about taking your life?"

Charlotte cut her eyes at him. "Never. I've been through things that I imagine would curl your toes. But I'm a survivor." *And proud of it.* "I'm just at a low point right now. I let my finances get out of control, and then after Ryan broke up with me, I knew I needed to make some changes. But never, ever would I consider taking my own life."

"That's *gut* to know." He stared straight ahead for a

few moments. "I reckon you could say I was depressed after Edna and I broke up, but I never felt like I couldn't go on."

Charlotte scowled. "Uh . . . are you referring to Edna *Glick*?" Charlotte cringed as she recalled the woman who'd played a role in Ethan's death. At least in Charlotte's mind, she did.

"Do you know her?"

"Yeah. I know her all right." Charlotte snarled in his direction.

"What did Edna ever do to you?"

Charlotte wondered if she should tread lightly since Daniel's tone was a little defensive. She decided against it.

"Edna had a relationship with my brother and ultimately broke his heart." Right away, she thought about Hannah. As far as most people knew, Hannah was the one Ethan had loved.

"And you blame her for your brother's death?"

Ethan's depression had taken him at the end, but it was so much easier for Charlotte to blame the woman he'd been in love with. She glanced at Daniel. It looked like he might be gritting his teeth.

"I know it's not logical to blame Edna for my brother's death. Ethan's choices were his own, but . . ." Charlotte shrugged.

Daniel turned and stared out the window, the wind blowing his cropped bangs to one side. He'd removed his hat not far into their trip.

"Good grief. How many people was that woman dating?"

Daniel turned toward her, his eyebrows furrowed, his jaw clenched. "I'm sorry for the loss of your *bruder*, but it's not like you think. I dated Edna long before Ethan ever showed up in our community. I didn't know about her involvement with your *bruder*. I'd heard talk of it, even suspected it, but I didn't know for sure until now."

Charlotte wanted to let it go, to change the subject, but she was having trouble picturing Daniel with Edna in a romantic way, which was silly since she didn't know either of them very well. "You can tell me it's none of my business, but what happened with you and Edna?" She scratched her nose, which tickled from the earlier blast of dust they'd taken in on the dirt and gravel roads.

Daniel turned toward her. "It's none of your business." He grinned, then chuckled when Charlotte scowled. "I don't really know. I thought we were happy, but she started to get distant, and the next thing I knew, she was spending time with John."

"And later with my brother," Charlotte added since that cat had already jumped out of the bag. Daniel winced.

"I'm sorry. I shouldn't have said anything about Edna and Ethan."

Daniel shrugged. "It's okay. I thought the rumors might be true. I don't think Edna is a happy person." He got a faraway look in his eyes as compassion seemed to replace either anger or hurt. Charlotte wasn't sure what he was feeling, but Edna's happiness wasn't her concern.

"I have a picture of Edna and me together, and even in the photo, she isn't smiling."

Charlotte stared at him and shook her head. "I don't get it. I thought pictures weren't allowed. I thought cell phones weren't allowed either, but all of you seem to have one, even Hannah." She held up a hand when Daniel opened his mouth to interrupt. "Don't get me wrong. I love Hannah and her family, and Lancaster County is my favorite place. But I just worry that you'll . . ." She paused. "I worry you'll end up like us, your *Englisch* friends, as you call us."

Daniel didn't crack a smile. "We worry about that, too, and I promise you, none of us want that to happen." He winked at her.

She grinned. He was witty. Under different circumstances, Charlotte might have been taken in by his tall stance, his muscular shoulders, and the way his gray eyes took on a bluish hue in the sunlight. But she was done with men for a while. *Not to mention, he's Amish.*

"I hope Annie is okay." Daniel stared straight ahead. He pulled out a small hand-sketched map from his pocket. "And I hope she agrees to come home." He marked a spot on the map with his finger.

"At least she is with a relative."

Daniel laughed. "*Ya*, she's with a relative. A wacky relative."

Annie looked on while her aunt danced around the living room, humming and using a feather duster on her furniture. Plumes of dust swirled in the air, only to settle in a new place. Aunt Faye had been good to Annie since she'd arrived, trying to tend to her every need. She'd told Annie that she hadn't had any paying tenants in a while. But when their first meal together consisted of a peanut butter and mayonnaise sandwich with a side of raw cabbage, Annie could see why. She wasn't sure if it was due to her condition or the food, but she worried she would hurl at any moment. But for dessert they'd had apple pie. And somehow her aunt had turned apple pie into the tastiest dessert Annie had ever put in her mouth.

But this morning's breakfast had been an odd one. Two fried eggs, sunny side up—which might have been tasty without the glob of sour cream on top—and a side of fried okra. Annie loved fried okra, but she could tell it was the frozen kind from a bag. And she'd never had it mixed together with warm grape jelly, and that hadn't sat well with her tummy either. But Aunt Faye seemed happy to have Annie here, so she forced herself to eat at least some of the food offerings so as not to hurt her aunt's feelings.

"Is there anything I can do to help you, Aunt Faye?" Annie spoke above the loud piano music playing in the background. Her aunt wore clothes similar to Annie's, but Mennonites were allowed to wear colorful designs on their dresses. Aunt Faye's light blue dress had a pastel flower print. She wore a prayer covering, although it wasn't in the traditional heart shape like in Lancaster County. It was flatter in the front, more like Ohio Amish wore.

"You just rest, dear." Faye carried the feather duster with her around the corner when the telephone rang. She returned a few moments later. "Jacob is on the phone for you."

Annie considered not taking the call, but Faye had already informed her that Jacob had returned to Paradise. Lena had told her that when Faye called to let everyone know Annie was okay. She'd had some time to think on things, and while she wasn't ready to face her family, she was interested to hear what Jacob had to say.

"*Wie bischt*, Annie. I miss you. Please come home." Jacob had something crunchy in his mouth, like chips. Annie frowned.

"I'm very upset, Jacob."

"I know. I heard what happened with your folks. But we just need to get married, and everything will be okay. Why didn't you tell me about the baby?" *Crunch, crunch, crunch.*

"I don't know, Jacob. I guess I didn't want you to feel trapped."

She waited for him to deny that he would ever feel that way, but just heard more crunching.

Annie huffed. "Can you at least talk to me without a mouthful of food?"

"I'm hungry. Sorry."

They were quiet. Annie was trying to imagine a life with Jacob. Everything felt different now. He'd broken her trust when he left her, and now the little things were bothering her too. Like talking with his mouth full.

"I might have considered marrying you for the sake of our child." She paused as she tried to briefly envision life as a single mother. "But I'm not sure you would be happy, Jacob."

"You're having our baby. We will make it work, *ya*?"

That wasn't exactly what Annie wanted to hear. *Maybe because you love me?* "Well, I still don't know."

"Daniel and Charlotte are on their way there."

"What?" Annie put a hand to her forehead. "Why can't everyone just give me some time to myself? And why is Charlotte coming?"

"She can drive."

If Annie married Jacob, her parents would be happy. She figured Jacob's family would be happy too. But would she? Would Jacob?

Annie was still pondering that when someone knocked on the front door. "They're here. I have to go." She hung up the phone, rounded the corner into the living room, and folded her hands in front of her. She held her breath as Aunt Faye ushered Daniel and Charlotte into her living room. Then her aunt walked across the room and removed the needle from the record player, halting the background music. She rejoined the group, introduced herself to Charlotte, then hugged Daniel.

"I'm going to let you all talk privately." She pointed down the hallway. "I'll be in the cemetery room if you need me."

Annie waited until her aunt was out of earshot before she whispered, "That's a room where she has all the mementos from people she's lost—photographs, keepsakes, and such." She shook her head and sighed. "I don't know why she calls it her cemetery room, though."

Daniel turned to Charlotte and grinned. "See what I mean? Wacky." Then he walked to Annie and hugged her tightly. "*Mei maedel*, you scared us all. I know *Daed* was rough on you, but you belong at home."

Annie eased out of her brother's embrace and turned to Charlotte. "Sorry about your couch." Annie knew Jacob had already told Charlotte what really happened. Part of her wished Jacob had protected her, but she guessed she deserved it for being nasty.

"It's just a couch." Charlotte pinched her lips together in a smile that didn't look genuine. "Just glad you are safe and okay."

"Go and thank Aunt Faye for letting you stay the night, then we can be on our way back home." Daniel looked down the hallway, then back at Annie.

"I'm not going home." She folded her arms across her chest.

"*Ya*, you are," Daniel said. "Get your purse and let's go. I'm sure Jacob will marry you now that he's back." He paused. "You did know that he's home, *ya*?"

"I know. And he called me. But I don't know if I want to marry him anymore."

Daniel brought a hand to his forehead as he took a step toward her. "You have to."

"She doesn't *have* to, Daniel." Charlotte locked eyes with Annie. "No one can force you to get married if you don't want to." She tucked her long dark hair behind her ears. Annie was still getting used to seeing it flowing freely and not covered by a *kapp*.

Daniel's eyes blazed as he turned to Charlotte. "She must marry Jacob. It's the right thing to do."

"It's her life. Her decision."

"She's seventeen and pregnant. She must marry Jacob!"

Annie glanced back and forth between Charlotte and her brother as they both got louder. Her eyes landed back on Daniel. "You sound like *Daed*."

"Did Jacob say he wanted to marry you?" Daniel lifted his eyebrows.

"*Ya*, but I don't have to say yes."

"That's right." Charlotte gave a taut nod of her head, only to have Daniel cut his eyes at her.

"This is not your business, Charlotte." Daniel's voice grew even louder. Annie was surprised her aunt hadn't come to check things out, but she wasn't sure her aunt's hearing was all that good. The music earlier had sounded mighty loud to Annie.

Daniel's face was bright red as he pointed a finger at Charlotte. "Stop discouraging her from doing the right thing."

Charlotte glowered at him. "Was sleeping together before marriage the right thing? No. But now there is a baby coming, and if she and Jacob aren't totally committed to each other, they will all be miserable, and that's no way for a child to grow up. Believe me, I know."

Annie stepped sideways until she was right next to her new ally, both of them facing off with her brother.

Charlotte turned to her. "Annie, do you love Jacob? At one point, you must have—you were ready to get married in the fall."

Annie dipped her chin and stared at the floor before looking back at Charlotte. "I thought I did, but I don't know how I feel anymore."

"Well, maybe you just need to sit down with Jacob and talk things through."

In Annie's heart, she'd already made up her mind. "Jacob has no idea what he wants." She raised her palms. "One minute, he doesn't love me enough. After that, he wants to live in the *Englisch* world, then he doesn't. Then he finds out I'm pregnant and wants to marry me." She shook her head. "I—I don't know if I want to marry him, but I need . . ." She covered her face with her hands and started to cry. "Maybe Daniel is right, that I must marry my baby's father."

"*Ya*, you should." Daniel waved his arm toward the door. "Now let's go."

Annie swiped at her eyes, her legs trembling. She'd be going back to her parents' house, and everyone would try to convince her to get married. She needed more time to think. She turned to Charlotte.

"I want to stay with my aunt Faye awhile longer so I can think about things."

Charlotte opened her mouth to speak but clamped it shut and looked at Daniel.

"*Nee*, you may not!" Daniel stomped one foot. "Charlotte provided a ride. She is not part of the decision making!"

"Hey, quit yelling," Charlotte said, then she sighed and turned to Annie. "He's right. This is a family matter."

Daniel walked toward them. "Annie, I am not leaving here without you."

Annie walked to the floral couch, sat down, and raised her chin. "Suit yourself."

Daniel walked to a chair, sat down, and folded his arms across his chest.

Charlotte stared at them both. "Well, I guess you can both sit here and figure it out. I'll be outside sitting in that fine truck we arrived in."

After the door closed behind Charlotte, Annie walked to her brother and knelt on the floor in front of his chair. "Please, Daniel . . . I'm begging you. Let me just stay here for a little while."

Daniel shook his head.

But then Aunt Faye emerged from her cemetery room, and somehow Annie knew everything would be okay. Maybe it was because she had a baseball bat slung over one shoulder.

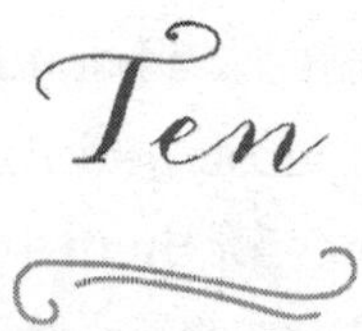

Charlotte ground the truck into gear after Daniel climbed in and slammed the door closed.

He put his hat in his lap and shook his head. "That woman is *ab im kopp.*" He turned to Charlotte, scowling. "That means 'crazy.'"

"I know what it means." She grinned, but only a little since he was so red in the face. "I retained a little Pennsylvania Dutch from my last visit."

"She threatened me with a baseball bat. No wonder we don't visit her much."

Charlotte finished shifting gears again, then put a hand to her mouth to cover her amusement. Her eyes veered in Daniel's direction, and his face was as red as the truck they were in. But she burst out laughing.

He raised both eyebrows, but his expression was flat.

"I'm sorry," she said. "I'm just trying to picture your

sweet aunt Faye swinging a baseball bat at you. I thought your people were passive."

"*Ya*, exactly."

After a little while, Charlotte said, "I'm sorry about getting involved. It's just . . . a bad marriage can have lasting effects on a child. Jacob and Annie have to really be committed to each other for them to have a good marriage and be good parents. But I should have stayed out of it."

Daniel stroked his chin. "It's just not our way. If Jacob and Annie are old enough to do what they did, then they should be old enough to act responsibly and get married."

"My mom was pregnant with me when she married my dad. And it was a match made in—" She paused. "Let's just say I would have been better off if they hadn't gotten married, or if I would have been raised by a crazy, bat-wielding aunt."

Daniel grinned. "Aunt Faye is the exception to every rule. She's not Amish anymore either."

"And another thing. Remember what it was like to be seventeen? If someone tells you not to do something, it's usually exactly what you'll fight to do. Hopefully, Jacob and Annie will come to the best decision together. I'll pray that they do."

"*Ya*, I know. But who knows what nonsense Aunt Faye will tell Annie. And even more of a worry is whether or not *mei* great-aunt is mentally stable. Will Annie be safe there?"

Charlotte grinned. "Well . . . crazy Aunt Faye seemed mighty protective of Annie. I'm sure she'll be fine."

"I hope so."

Charlotte wrestled the big steering wheel to the left to make a turn, and once they were straightened out, she said, "You really love Annie."

"*Ya*. Very much. She acts like a five-year-old sometimes, though."

"I loved Ethan very much too. Even though we weren't close toward the end."

Daniel slapped a hand to his knee. "Your *haus*. We need to at least get the water mopped up before those floors start to buckle."

"Uh, I figured you might be too mad at me to help me with that." She rolled her lips into a pout, then sighed.

"I *am* mad at you."

She jerked her head his way. He was grinning.

"But I'll still fix your plumbing. I said I would, and I don't lie or break promises."

Charlotte wasn't sure if that was a dig at her past lies. She wondered if Daniel knew how hard she worked at not lying. How hard she strived to be a better person each day, even if it was just a little better than the day before. If Charlotte had a worst enemy, it was herself.

Daniel and Charlotte stopped at Walmart on their way home. Charlotte gathered some towels and a mop. Daniel tried to buy the parts to repair the plumbing at Ethan's house—Charlotte's house—but she insisted on paying for everything. But while she mopped up water, Daniel stumbled upon a larger problem.

"It's not just that the fittings have come loose," he said as he met up with her in the living room. "One of the pipes running underneath the house is cracked, I think."

Charlotte turned pale.

Daniel wasn't sure he would have offered to repair her plumbing if he'd known it was going to be such a big problem. But Charlotte looked like she might cry again.

"I—I mean, I can fix it. I just don't have the right tools with me," he said as he took a step closer to her. "I need to go let my parents know about Annie. Then I can come back when I have time, with the right tools and parts."

"No, no." She sighed. "I can't let you do that. I'll get it handled."

Daniel thought for a moment. God would surely be disappointed in him if he walked away from an opportunity to help someone. "Hiring a plumber to do the work will be expensive."

Her eyes widened. "Like, how expensive?"

"The water is turned off. It will take a few days for the floors to dry out, but they should be okay. Call your real estate person and maybe ask her not to show the house right now. And as soon as I can, I will make the repairs."

She walked to him, and without any warning, she wrapped her arms around his waist. Daniel kept his arms to his sides at first, unsure what to make of this unexpected display of emotion.

"Thank you, thank you," she said as she squeezed him around his waist.

He patted her on the back, then eased away. "It's not a problem."

Charlotte dropped him off at home fifteen minutes later. She was an odd duck, the *Englisch* woman. Her sense of gratitude over a small thing was touching, if not a little extreme. It was just a house, just a broken pipe. But he supposed that for Charlotte that house must represent a way to fix her life, financially anyway. Daniel wanted to dislike her since he didn't really trust her—or appreciate her butting into family business. But there was something about Charlotte that he liked. He pushed aside the fact that she was beautiful. Daniel had never been one to size up a person by looks alone. *Nee*, there was something else about Charlotte that stoked Daniel's interest.

He returned home and faced off with his father the moment he walked in the door. His mother stood at the far end of the living room.

"Where is Annie?"

"She's not coming back yet." Daniel hung his hat on

the rack by the door, bracing himself for what was sure to come.

Mamm raced toward him. "Why? She must! Jacob wants to marry her."

Daniel's father held a palm up. "Eve, shush." He turned back to Daniel. "You are her *bruder*, her much older *bruder*. Why didn't you make her come back?"

Daniel was angry with his father for being so hard on Annie, but he held his tongue as best he could. "What would you have wanted me to do? Hit her over the head? Drag her kicking and screaming all the way home?" *Or get beaten over the head with a baseball bat?*

"You watch yourself," his father said, narrowing his eyes at Daniel.

"She left because of you." Daniel instinctively took a step backward when his father stepped forward. Lucas Byler had never laid a hand on either of his children. Daniel had taken many trips to the woodshed for whippings, but always at the hand of his mother—a woman who had turned into a shadow all of a sudden.

"Maybe she just needs some time to think, like Jacob did," his mother said. "Then she'll come home and do the right thing."

Daed threw his arms up. "What is it with everyone needing to go away to think? And I can't imagine a worse place for her to go than to your aunt Faye's house. That woman is a lunatic."

Daniel agreed but decided not to anger his father

further by mentioning the baseball bat. He shrugged. "Annie wouldn't come back. I tried."

~

Jacob walked across the yard to where Hannah was taking clothes from the line.

"Why are you doing clothes on Wednesday?" Everyone knew Monday was wash day.

"We've been worried about you, and everything is off schedule."

Jacob had just seen Hannah and Isaac chatting outside earlier, so hopefully his sister was in a good mood and could help him sort out the mess in his head. He looped his thumbs beneath his suspenders and waited until she'd folded a pair of slacks and laid them in the basket. When she looked up at him, she shook her head.

"What's that for, the head shaking?"

"Because I know you." Hannah turned back to the clothes and unpinned a maroon dress from the line.

"What is it you think you know?"

She looked at him. "You don't want to marry Annie, but you're going to anyway because everyone wants you to and because it's the right thing to do." She laid the dress in the basket on top of the slacks, then stopped and faced Jacob. "I can't imagine for one minute my life without Isaac, and I'm counting the days until we get married in the fall. He is everything to me. I want to close my eyes at night knowing that Isaac loves me with all his heart, and wake up with him each morning knowing that I feel exactly the same way."

Jacob frowned. "What makes you think I don't want that same thing?"

"I'm not saying you don't *want* the same thing. But do you have that with Annie?" Hannah took down another pair of slacks from the line.

He was afraid to voice his true feelings, so he kicked at the grass, trying to decide if being truthful with Hannah would make him feel better or worse. "I love Annie. She's a *gut* person, probably the best person for me to marry, especially since she's pregnant."

"Um, okay . . ." Hannah sounded doubtful.

"When I'm with Annie, I'm not sure I want to be with her forever. When I'm not with her, I miss her." He shook his head. "It doesn't make sense. And I'm still not sure that I don't want to be in the *Englisch* world. I'm all confused."

Hannah dropped the pants she was holding, gasped, and then slammed a hand to her mouth.

"What's wrong with you?" Jacob narrowed his eyebrows, then wiped at his mouth, wondering if something big and green was in his teeth. "What are you looking at?"

Without moving her hand from her mouth, she pointed . . . at his arm.

"What have you done?" Hannah finally edged closer, peeking underneath his short-sleeved shirt, only to jump back so fast you'd have thought the tattoo fired a lightning rod at her.

He rolled his sleeve up so Hannah could see the whole tattoo.

His sister backed up, fell over the laundry basket, and landed in the grass.

"This is my souvenir from Houston," Jacob crowed.

"Who, who . . ." Hannah sounded like an owl. "Who did that to your arm?"

Jacob stood taller, grinning. "An *Englisch* man in a tattoo shop. Do you like it?"

Hannah stood up and brushed grass from her apron, keeping her eyes on Jacob's tattoo. "*Mamm* and *Daed* are going to go bonkers when they see that."

Jacob tugged the sleeve of his shirt down as much as he could, although the tip of the crescent moon still showed. He needed to wear long-sleeved shirts until he was ready to tell his parents about the tattoo. "What do you think I should do?"

She grimaced. "About the tattoo or Annie?"

"I can't do anything about the tattoo—even if I wanted to, which I don't—so I guess Annie."

Hannah put her hands on her hips. "First of all, shame on you and Annie for letting your hormones get the best of you."

"It only happened once, and—"

"Apparently, that's all it takes." Hannah held up a finger when Jacob opened his mouth to speak. "And secondly, where you go from here is a decision you and Annie have to make."

Jacob exhaled loudly. "She's saying she doesn't know if she wants to marry me anymore."

"Can't say that I blame her. You left her, came back, and don't seem to know if you even want to be Amish." Hannah picked up the laundry basket, and Jacob got in step with her on the way back to the house. "I guess we'll all find out soon enough when Daniel returns with Annie."

Jacob didn't say anything.

Charlotte quietly closed her computer, hoping not to wake up Hannah. She missed having Buddy sleep at the foot of her bed, but her trusted companion had taken to sleeping on Amos and Lena's bed. Lena often went to bed before her husband, and Buddy spent much of his time curled up in Amos's lap in the evenings. But when Amos headed to bed, Buddy followed him. If Buddy had chosen anyone else over Charlotte, she might have been upset. But she suspected Buddy felt the same way as Charlotte when it came to Amos. The need to feel his love.

She extinguished the flame on the lantern, surprised by how easily she'd settled back into a life without electricity. As she nestled under the covers, thoughts of the woman and girl from her dream briefly entered her mind, but the recollection no longer caused her head to throb or her chest to ache. Whatever physical response she'd been having seemed to be gone. From there her thoughts turned to Annie. She wondered if Ethan would have reacted so radically if he and Charlotte were in Daniel and Annie's situation. Rolling onto her side, she decided it wasn't comparing apples to apples.

She jumped when her cell phone vibrated on the nightstand. As she studied the number, she scurried out of bed to the hallway. It wasn't a number she recognized, but it was a local area code. She was at the stairs when she answered in a whisper.

"Oops. I woke you. This is Daniel."

They'd exchanged numbers before Charlotte dropped him off at home, but she was surprised he was calling. "No, I wasn't asleep," she said in a whisper. "I'm going downstairs so I don't wake up Hannah. Hang on a minute." She tiptoed down the stairs, clutching the handrail, then felt her way around until she found the couch and a small amount of light coming from the solar lamp in the yard. *Too close to Lena and Amos's room.* She went to the kitchen, hoping Buddy wouldn't start barking, and found a flashlight. She eased a kitchen chair out as quietly as she could and sat down. "Okay, I can talk easier now. Is everything okay?" She swirled the flashlight in circles on the ceiling above her head.

"*Ya*. Well . . . mostly."

Charlotte stilled the flashlight. "What's wrong?"

"*Ach*, nothing really."

Charlotte waited. *Why are you calling me?* When the silence became a little awkward, Charlotte asked, "So, um . . . how did it go with your parents when you got home? I'm sure they were upset Annie wasn't with you."

"*Ya*, my homecoming went as I expected."

Charlotte wondered why Daniel still lived at home. He was a year younger than Charlotte. She recalled Annie saying he was twenty-five. "I think Annie will want to go home after a few days."

"*Mei daed* is a *gut* man. But this situation with Annie has him worked up more than I've ever seen him. I know a father worries about his *kinner*, but he's going overboard with Annie, and I'm afraid she won't want to come home because of that."

Charlotte reminded herself that the Amish had their own set of traditional values, but comingled with that thought was her own upbringing. "I know everyone is upset and worried about the decisions facing Annie and Jacob, but it has to be the right thing for them. A bad marriage with unhappy people is not a good environment for a child. You got mad at me when I said that before, but it's true."

"Jacob and Annie are young. If they don't have the kind of love for marriage now, they will grow into it."

"It doesn't always work that way. But I'm not going to say anything more to either one of them about it. They have to make their own decisions. But Daniel,

Annie does have choices, and you shouldn't influence her either."

He was quiet, and Charlotte assumed she'd overstepped.

Daniel cleared his throat. "I should have protected Annie better, been a better *bruder* to her. Maybe she wouldn't be in this mess."

"She's in this mess because Jacob couldn't keep his—" She stopped, knowing it takes two to tango. "You couldn't have stopped her. They are two teenagers who got caught up in the moment and acted on it."

"I don't know . . ."

Charlotte heard the regret in his voice, still surprised he'd chosen her to confide in. "If Annie and Jacob get married, do they have a place to live? Because I can offer them a great deal on a little blue house in the area." She set the flashlight in motion on the ceiling again.

"*Ya*, they would need a home."

A prospect. She reminded herself to call the realty company in the morning about the water being off and the repairs Daniel was going to make. "Why do you still live at home?" she asked since the topic provided a natural segue.

"I'm not married."

"I know. But don't you want to be out on your own?"

"Of course. But I've saved almost every penny I've earned since I started working when I was fourteen. For eleven years I've split my time between my part-time job building storage sheds and working the farm. I give *Mamm* and *Daed* some of it to help with expenses, and I've saved the rest. There was a time when I thought Edna and I might get married, and I was going to buy her the grandest house in Paradise. But that didn't work out. And I'm not dating anyone." He chuckled. "There's no one left to date. People in our community get married young."

Charlotte knew that to be true. "I'm sure you'll find someone."

"Now isn't a *gut* time with *Mamm* pregnant. Do you know how that works?"

"Uh . . ." *What is he asking me?*

He laughed again. Daniel had a nice laugh. Especially compared to Ryan, who made a weird gurgling sound when he laughed. She realized that the Jacob and Annie drama had kept thoughts of Ryan at bay.

"I didn't word that very *gut*," he said, then chuckled again. "I know how babies are made. I'm just wondering how dangerous it is for *mei mamm* to be having a baby at fifty-two. She's been sick a lot and vomiting, and I know that's normal, but when *Daed* told us she was with child, I could see the worry on his face. I didn't even know that could happen at her age."

"Most of the time, I don't think it does. But I'm sure her doctor will keep a close eye on her."

"Um . . . that is kind of why I'm calling."

Ah, finally.

"*Mamm*'s doctor called in a prescription for her. It's in Lancaster at the Walmart on Lincoln Highway, and our driver is still ill." He paused. "Is there a chance that you might be traveling that way in the next day or two? I—I mean, I was wondering if you might be able to pick up *Mamm*'s prescription. I'm sure you don't care for driving that truck, but I thought maybe—"

"I don't mind at all. As a matter of fact, I've been having trouble with my computer cord charging my computer, so I was going to have to make a trip to Lancaster anyway. Only thing is, I can't go until Friday. I promised Hannah and Isaac that I would take them to run errands for their wedding tomorrow. I'd be happy to pick up your mother's prescription if it doesn't have to be done tomorrow. Or I could drive to Lancaster late tomorrow afternoon. The places Hannah needs to go aren't near Lancaster, but if your mom needs the medicine tomorrow, I'll sure make the trip for her."

"*Nee*, Friday will be fine. *Danki*. I appreciate it, and I know *Mamm* will be grateful too. Annie was sick for a few days, but that was it. And nothing like the way *Mamm* is sick."

Charlotte yawned. "Some women don't have morning sickness or have a light case of it, like Annie."

They were quiet for a while, then Daniel spoke up.

"I want to apologize to you. You've been kind to Jacob and Annie, and whether or not I agreed with what you said to Annie, I had no right to yell at you. Especially at a time when you are enduring so much change in your life and hurting from a breakup."

"I appreciate that. Broken hearts heal. It just takes time, I suppose."

"I hurt over Edna for a long time, but . . ." He was quiet for a few moments. "I'm better. I hope you'll feel better soon too."

"Thank you." Charlotte yawned again as she made larger circles on the ceiling. Maybe she'd sneak a piece of buttered bread and a glass of milk since she was here. She was getting ready to say good night when Daniel spoke again.

"Can I ask you something?"

Charlotte shined the flashlight around the counter until she found a loaf of bread wrapped in plastic wrap. "Okay . . ."

"Why didn't you just ask Hannah and her family what happened instead of pretending to be Amish to get answers about your brother's death?"

Charlotte slumped into her chair and laid the flashlight on the table. She knew she hadn't imagined Daniel's hostility when she'd first arrived. This must be at the core of his thoughts of her.

"Well . . . at the time, I was convinced that the Amish people were some sort of cult that had lured my brother in and ultimately caused his suicide. I needed someone to blame. And I thought Hannah and her family were hiding something. It wasn't until I got to know them all that I realized how much they were hurting and how they didn't understand why Ethan did what he did either."

Daniel was quiet, then asked, "Do you think Edna had anything to do with Ethan's suicide?"

Charlotte squeezed her eyes tight. "You know, I really shouldn't have told you about Ethan and Edna. I'm not normally a gossip. And to be honest, I think Ethan might have been a bit obsessed with Edna, and that combined with his depression is what may have sent him over the edge. Edna chose John over Ethan. I didn't know that you had dated her too." Charlotte didn't care much for the woman, but she'd already made that clear to Daniel. "It makes me feel better to blame someone occasionally, even if I know the blame is misdirected at Edna."

"Hmm . . . I think Edna is a little lost right now. She doesn't seem happy with John. Or maybe she's upset about something else."

"Depression is a tricky type of illness, and I think it's hard to diagnose sometimes."

"I'm sorry about your brother. I really am. I don't know what I'd do if anything happened to Annie. I feel so responsible for her, even though I know that she will follow her own path. I just hope she chooses wisely."

"Thank you for saying that about Ethan. I hope Annie chooses what is best for her and her baby." Charlotte stifled another yawn.

"I'll let you get some sleep. Thank you again for saying you'd pick up *Mamm*'s prescription."

"No problem. I'll drop it off Friday." She wondered how much it would cost, knowing Daniel would pay her back, but also hoping she had enough money up front.

"And I hope things go well with the sale of your house. I should have the plumbing problems fixed tomorrow, I hope."

"Thank you so much for helping me with this. Did you notice if the mattress was in the bedroom?"

"*Nee*, I was just looking for where the water was coming in, kitchen or bathroom. I didn't really pay attention to anything else."

"Isaac had planned to give the bed to a family who needed it, but the mattress has a big stain on it now. A stain that wasn't there a couple of weeks ago. It looks like someone spilled a soda. I told Hannah that maybe kids have been going in there. We found a couple of windows unlocked, but Hannah and I made sure everything was locked when we left."

"I go right by there most days. Do you want me to check on the place?"

Charlotte smiled. "That's really nice of you to offer. But I can drive over there."

"*Ach*, okay. I just thought you might not like going there, since Ethan . . ."

. . . hanged himself from a tree in the yard. "If it's on

your way, and if it's no trouble, maybe you could just take a peek now and then."

"Even after I repair the plumbing, I can go by a couple times a week if it doesn't sell right away. I have the key you gave me."

"Thank you very much. I'm trying to get caught up on my work, and I'm also trying to help out Hannah and Lena while I'm staying with them. And as for Annie, I really do think that she will be homesick after a few days, and she'll be missing Jacob. She's just scared and confused. And young."

"I hope you're right. And maybe *mei daed* will have some time to calm down."

"I guess I should probably say good night." Yawning, she stilled the flashlight. "You know what they say—everything will be well in the end. If it's not well, it's not the end."

"I like that. Good night, Charlotte."

After Charlotte hung up, she made her way to the counter and was unwrapping the bread when she heard footsteps shuffling across the living room toward the kitchen. She shined the flashlight in that direction.

"Jacob, what are you doing up?" It was only nine thirty, but usually everyone but Charlotte was sound asleep by now.

"I heard someone downstairs, and I figured it was you," he said in a whisper as he tiptoed toward her. "I've been afraid to come downstairs, that I'll wake your dog, but I need to talk to you, and I couldn't wait any longer."

She stopped fumbling with the loaf of bread and leaned against the counter, the flashlight shining near his face. "What's wrong?"

"*Everything* is wrong. Everything, Charlotte. Can we please talk?"

Charlotte was unsure when she became a counselor for wayward teens, but she nodded, hoping she could stay true to what she'd told Daniel—that she wouldn't influence Annie or Jacob.

Eleven

Jacob was pretty sure the weight of the world had landed on his shoulders, and the pressure was squashing him an inch at a time. Soon he'd be a puddle of mush on the floor if he didn't get his head and heart aligned.

"Everyone is telling me I have to marry Annie," he told Charlotte in a loud whisper. "I want to be a *gut* father. I really do. I want to be a *gut* husband too. But I feel . . . trapped." He paused, but when Charlotte didn't say anything, he said, "What should I do?"

"Jacob, I can't tell you what to do. But I can tell you that Annie is having doubts about marrying you too."

"I know." Jacob scratched his forehead as he settled into a kitchen chair. "So it doesn't seem like we should get married then. Right?"

"I think the two of you need to talk in person, but Annie doesn't want to see or talk to you or her family yet."

"I know. I've tried calling lots of times."

"I think she will want to come home soon. When she does, the two of you can decide what's best for both of you and your baby."

"What if we want different things?"

"It is starting to sound like neither one of you wants to get married, but maybe things will look better in the morning."

Jacob was pretty sure they wouldn't. He was quiet while Charlotte buttered herself a piece of bread. She leaned against the counter and took a big bite, then yawned. Nothing was going to get decided tonight, so he slathered butter on a piece of bread for himself, and when they were both done, Jacob thanked her for listening and tiptoed across the living room. He'd hoped Charlotte would offer advice. Everyone wanted to offer an opinion, it seemed, but so far no one had told Jacob what he wanted to hear.

After he was back upstairs, he looked underneath the bed at his packed suitcase. It gave him comfort to be ready, even though he didn't know where he'd go or what he'd do. But he'd forge ahead and leave if the walls got any tighter around him.

∽

Despite his worries about Annie, Daniel started his day the same way he always did, if not a bit later than normal. He dressed, ate breakfast with his parents, fed the horses and cows, milked their only goat, and gathered eggs for *Mamm*. Normally his mother would take care of the goat and eggs, but the barnyard smells didn't sit well with her now that she was with child, so Daniel had taken over a few things for her.

He was meeting Bill Morgan at the job site. They were building a small storage shed for an *Englisch* fellow. Daniel had worked for Bill long enough to know that Bill would be at least thirty minutes late. His *Englisch* employer couldn't seem to get going without two donuts and a cup of coffee, and Bill never accounted for that stop when he set a time to start. Daniel decided to check on Charlotte's house. He didn't have time to do the repairs until later in the day, but he could at least check the floors. He pulled the key from his pocket but checked the doorknob first to make sure it was locked. It wasn't.

Slowly, he entered the living room. "Hello?" He walked into the kitchen, the smell of fresh paint giving him an instant headache, like it had the last time he was here. When he touched the wood floors, they were damp, but much drier than before. He crossed through the living room and into the bedroom, which was empty except for the bed. He noticed the stain Charlotte mentioned. Perhaps the real estate agent had accidently left the door unlocked. Although it seemed odd that someone would have come last night or so early this morning. Hopefully Charlotte had called the real estate people and halted the showings until Daniel finished the repairs. He double-checked the windows and the back door, then locked the front door as he left. He slowed down as he crossed the yard, glancing at the massive oak tree. As he got back in the buggy, he thought about Annie, praying she would make good choices.

Friday morning, Annie woke up two hours before her aunt emerged from her bedroom. She made some toast and found an apple, and the minute Aunt Faye started rattling pans in the kitchen, Annie was quick to let her aunt know she'd already eaten.

Annie was grateful that the few days of throwing up hadn't lasted. It must have been a stomach virus, and she was glad that she didn't have to deal with all these life decisions *and* morning sickness too. But her aunt's cooking and choice of ingredient combos might make anyone throw up. She thought about her mother again, knowing she should probably go home, if for no other reason than to be there for *Mamm*. It was her father keeping her away, but she needed to get her priorities straight.

"I should probably go home and marry Jacob," she said when Aunt Faye walked into the living room toting a plate, then sat down on the couch and put it in her lap.

"Are you sure you don't want some deviled oysters, dear?"

Annie shook her head fiercely. "*Nee*, *danki* though." She wondered if Aunt Faye knew her prayer covering was lopsided. Annie decided not to say anything.

Aunt Faye held up an egg filled presumably with pickled oysters. Annie had never had oysters, but she wasn't sure she wanted to try them for the first time pickled and for breakfast.

"I make these every week. There are some left that we can have with our pancakes tomorrow morning." She shoveled an egg into her mouth as Annie struggled not to cringe. Home was looking better and better. Annie excused herself to make a phone call.

Friday morning, Daniel stood on the porch waiting for Annie to get home. He had already decided to act as a buffer between his father and his sister, even though their father had calmed down considerably. Right now everyone needed to focus on *Mamm*, taking over some of her chores and making sure she didn't do too much, as the doctor had instructed. He sat down in one of the rocking chairs just as the screen door opened and his father stepped outside.

"She should be home soon, *ya*?"

"I think so," Daniel said, kicking the chair into motion. "She called an hour ago to say they were leaving soon."

Daed waved an arm in the air. "All this talking on phones must stop. Before you know it, we will be using electricity and driving automobiles. We'd be one with the *Englisch*." He glowered, shaking his head.

"*Daed*, Annie is strong willed, and she's going to do what she wants to do. If you try to force her and Jacob into marriage, they might be rebellious. Maybe they will come to that conclusion on their own."

His father stared across the yard, past the barn, and toward the acres of spring growth spreading in hues of yellow and green. "I have thought on this."

Daniel braced himself.

"And you are right," his father said. "I will give them a chance to make things right."

Relief rushed through Daniel.

"But I don't think that boy is right for Annie. He's too wishy-washy."

Daniel held back a grin. It wasn't a phrase he'd ever heard his father use, although he agreed with *Daed* completely. Jacob didn't know what he wanted. "I think we all just need to focus on *Mamm*. Everything else will work itself out." *One way or the other.*

Daed took a seat in the other rocker, crossing an ankle over one knee. "I can't tell how your *mamm* feels about having another baby. She keeps saying what a blessing it is, but sometimes I think she is trying to convince herself."

His mother was probably looking forward to

grandchildren—the kind of blessings you borrow and return, not another child to raise full-time. "I just hope there aren't any problems, that she does everything the doctor says."

"You and Annie were born right here in this house." His father's eyes beamed, as he nodded behind him. "But the *Englisch* doctor said this *boppli* must be born in a hospital."

"I think that's wise," Daniel said just as a car turned in the driveway. "There's Annie." He stood up, stuffed his hands in his pockets, and waited. "And Aunt Faye."

Daed shook his head. "Do you think she will want to come in?"

"*Ya*, I'm guessing so. She'll probably want to see *Mamm*." Hopefully Aunt Faye had left her baseball bat at home.

"That car looks like the ones they made before you were even born." *Daed* brought a hand to his forehead as he peered at the long green car.

"It's a station wagon," Daniel said as both car doors opened.

"I know that." *Daed* scowled at Daniel as he lowered his hand.

"*Gut* to have you back," Daniel said after Annie got out of the car, toting her suitcase.

Aunt Faye followed Annie across the yard, carrying a brown paper bag on her hip. His sister slowed her steps as she neared the porch, locking eyes with their father. But when *Daed* stood up and held out his arms to Annie, his sister dropped the suitcase and ran to him.

Daniel still saw Annie as a little girl, and he knew their father did too. Somewhere along the line, Annie had grown into a young woman. And now she was going to be a mother.

"You can thank me later," Aunt Faye said as she marched up the porch steps. "I've brought enough food to last you through the weekend, including some pickled oysters. Annie said Eve is pregnant, too, and I figure you boys probably aren't helping out one bit." She brushed past all of them and walked into the house.

Daniel was sure his mother would hurl if she got a whiff of pickled oysters.

It was midday on Friday when Annie opened the front door.

"I was glad to hear that you came home." Charlotte smiled.

"Daniel had to meet his boss about an installation, but he said you would be bringing *Mamm*'s medicine today. *Danki*, Charlotte."

She accepted the bag and motioned for Charlotte to come in. "No one is here right now, but *Mamm* left some money. How much was it?"

Charlotte told her the cost, and Annie paid her.

"How is Jacob?" Annie asked. "I thought he would be over here the instant he heard I was back home."

"I feel like he is probably as confused as you are. He's getting a lot of advice from everyone too."

"What do you think I should do? Should I marry him?" Annie couldn't believe she was asking an *Englisch* person she barely knew to chime in about a decision that would affect the rest of her life, but Charlotte had gone up against Daniel when her brother had tried to push her into marriage. Maybe Charlotte was exactly the person she needed to talk to, someone who would give Annie the answer she wanted to hear.

"I don't know. Only you and Jacob can decide."

"I guess I have to marry him." Tears pooled in the corners of her eyes. "Then both of our families will be happy, and our child will grow up with two parents." She dabbed her eyes with a tissue. "Do you think God is punishing us for what we did? I know a baby is a blessing, but having sex before marriage is wrong. And now we're having all these problems, and . . ." She shook her head.

"One thing I learned from my time living with the Kings, that isn't how God works. But when we're in the midst of a crisis, sometimes we feel like God has abandoned us or that we're unworthy of happiness. That's never His intent—we just can't foresee His plan for us."

~

Charlotte stared into space, realizing she was ministering to herself more than Annie, and she needed to heed her own advice. "When Ryan broke up with me, I was sure it was God turning away from me, that I didn't deserve to be happy. It hasn't been very long since we broke up, so it still hurts, but our breakup has forced me to really dissect our relationship to figure out what went wrong." She paused and took a deep breath. "Aside from the fact that he cheated on me."

Annie nodded, not crying so much. "I'm sorry you were hurt."

Charlotte shrugged. "Ryan's the first man I ever let into my heart, and it was hard for me to trust. I'm afraid it will be even harder for me to trust someone after his betrayal. But with each day, I heal a little more. No more thoughts about chopping him up with an ax while he sleeps."

Annie gasped, which made Charlotte laugh. "Annie, I'm kidding." Her cell phone rang in her purse, so she fumbled around until she found it. "It's your brother. I should probably answer it."

"Did you have any problems getting the prescription?" Daniel asked after she said hello.

"Nope, I brought your mom's medicine by your house, and I was just chatting with Annie." She glanced at Annie. The poor girl hung her head.

"*Gut*, thank you. I'm sure she's sitting right there so you can't really talk, but I wanted you to know that I checked on your house on my way in to work. Everything was fine, but the door was unlocked."

"Wow. Maybe Yvonne has already showed the house, but it would have been really early in the morning. I'll check with her and call you back shortly. I'd left her a message about the plumbing issues."

After she hung up, she turned back to Annie. "You're going to be okay, no matter what you and Jacob decide."

"I hope so." She spoke through tears, sniffling.

"Sweetie, what is it you're the most upset about? That Jacob really wants to marry you, not just because you're pregnant? That he may not want to? Your father? Of being a mom?"

"All of it. If I don't marry Jacob, I'll be alone with a baby. If I do marry him, I'll be with him the rest of my life." She sighed. "We don't get divorces. If we don't get married, it's my father's wrath I fear in the long run. I know *mei daed* just wanted me to come home, and so he is biting his tongue about this whole situation for the moment. And he doesn't want *mei mudder* upset again. And yes . . . I'm not really ready to have a *boppli*." She took a deep breath.

Charlotte had to admit, the girl had a lot to be concerned about, but all this upset surely wasn't good for the baby. "Pray about it, Annie. You'll make the right decision." Charlotte felt her phone vibrate in her purse. She pulled it out and eyed the number.

"I need to take this call. It's my real estate agent—we

keep playing phone tag. It'll only take a minute. Is that okay?"

"*Ya*, of course." Annie sniffled, then smoothed the wrinkles from her dress.

When Charlotte answered the phone, she told Yvonne about the door being unlocked.

"Hmm, that's unusual. I haven't showed the house," Yvonne said. "However . . . I did get an odd phone call from someone asking about your house."

"Odd how?"

"I haven't taken any pictures, so the listing is very basic, just stating the square footage based on the tax roll, the price, and the size of the lot. And I put in the listing that the house doesn't have electricity. But the caller—a woman—didn't ask any questions about the details of the home. Instead, she wanted to know if I knew the man who had lived there. I told her I did not know him. Then she thanked me and hung up."

"Hmm . . . a little odd, I guess." Charlotte hoped Ethan hadn't been involved with another woman. *Good grief.*

"We've set the price really low, so I think it'll go quick. But let me know when the plumbing repairs are taken care of."

They ended the call, and Charlotte was glad to see that Annie had stopped crying.

"Everything okay with your house?" she asked.

"Yeah, I think so. It's just kind of strange that a

random woman would ask the listing agent if she knew the owner, but then not want to know anything about the house." Charlotte paused. "Oh well. Maybe she'll call back and want to see it." She looked at Annie. "I should probably go, but are you going to be okay?"

Annie nodded. "*Ya, ya. Danki* for coming. I know I have a lot to think about." She smiled a little. "And I can tell you're trying not to influence me."

"Well, I'm *trying* not to. It seems important to your brother that I don't, and he's right. But you do have choices." Charlotte walked to the door, Annie following. "That's all I'm going to say. And now, it's time for me to get Big Red back home."

Annie followed her to the old truck. "Big Red?" Annie chuckled. "That name seems to fit."

Charlotte hugged her, happy that the girl had warmed up to her. But one thing still lingered in Charlotte's mind. As she eased away, she held Annie at arm's length. "I'm so sorry for all the lies I told last time I was here." It was all-consuming sometimes, Charlotte's need to be forgiven for her past choices. "Please forgive me."

Annie smiled. "I already did."

~

When his phone rang, Daniel excused himself from Bill and the other two men he was eating lunch with at the diner. He usually brought his lunch, so this was a treat to eat out, though it was later than he normally ate. He stepped onto the sidewalk outside the diner then walked around to the side of the building, feeling like a criminal. The *Englisch* always looked shocked when they saw an Amish person using a cell phone. They seemed to have preconceived notions about the way the Amish should and shouldn't be—almost like they felt cheated if the Amish weren't performing in the touristy capacity they expected.

"Hey. I talked to Yvonne, and she hasn't shown the house to anyone, so I don't know why the front door was unlocked. There's nothing to take, so I'm not going to worry about it right now."

"I'll keep my eyes open next time I go over there. How was your visit with Annie?"

"You'd have been proud of me. I did my best not to influence her." Daniel listened as she gave him details about their conversation.

"They wanted to get married before they knew Annie was pregnant," he said. "So I don't understand why everything is such a mess now."

"In a nutshell, I think Jacob feels trapped. And I think he felt that way before he even knew there was a baby. That's why he left in the first place. And Annie doesn't trust Jacob anymore."

Daniel paced back and forth, scratching his forehead. "Well, they need to get married. That's all there is to it."

"I disagree, but I've kept my promise not to sway either one of them."

"How can it possibly be *gut* for them not to get married? Annie would be raising a baby on her own, and how could Jacob bond with his child?"

"Because they will resent each other. As I told you before, my mom was pregnant with me when she married my father, and trust me, I wish they'd never gotten married. Ethan and I had a pretty rough childhood, and both of us eventually ended up in foster care."

Daniel recalled his and Annie's childhood. It hadn't been perfect, but there had always been love. "I'm sorry that your growing-up years weren't *gut*. But Jacob and Annie have created this situation, this baby, and they both need to be responsible now."

"It's a decision they need to make together."

Daniel didn't want to argue with Charlotte. He supposed if he had grown up the way she did, he might feel different.

"Is she feeling okay?" Daniel had heard his mother throwing up at home early this morning. "*Mei mamm* has been really sick."

"Annie seems okay—at least physically. Has your mother been to the doctor?"

"*Ya.* She will have to go often. And I think that's part of the reason *Daed* has been so hard on Annie; he's worried about *Mamm* too."

"There's a lot going on in your family right now. I will remember to keep you all in my prayers."

"*Danki.* I will keep you in my prayers, too, Charlotte.

You have been *gut* to Annie and Jacob. Do you have something specific you'd like me to pray for?"

~

Charlotte thought for a few moments. A week ago, she would have asked Daniel to pray that she'd become financially stable and for God to mend her broken heart. But as she watched Annie and Jacob struggling and also recalled her own childhood, she sensed her objectives beginning to shift. She was trying to accept that God hadn't abandoned her but was just guiding her in a new direction. But it was hard to understand why she couldn't find any peace.

"I guess, if I could ask you to pray for anything, it would be that I accept God's plan for my life. I don't have to understand it, but I need to trust it. God wants me to be happy, but I can't shake the feeling that I'm not deserving yet. I've made so many mistakes." She paused. "I know how that sounds, and I know in my heart that's not how God works, but . . ."

"Charlotte, I am going to pray for you every day, that God will guide you onto the path He has chosen for you, and that you will trust Him with all your heart."

She manhandled Big Red's steering wheel into the Kings' driveway, touched by the tenderness in Daniel's voice. "Thank you. I guess I have trust issues in general, even when it comes to my faith." She recalled the way she and Ryan used to pray together, before meals, and sometimes during the day if something was heavy on their hearts. When he'd broken up with her, she'd asked him to pray with her, that they could fix things. She'd never forget his expression, his teary eyes and blank gaze, as he said, "I already did," as if God had given him specific instructions to walk away from her, away from the life they'd planned. And all the while, he'd been cheating on her. Maybe she was meant to catch Ryan in the act, God's little nudge that he wasn't the right guy for her.

"I suppose it's hard for me to trust people, too, but I believe fiercely in God's will," Daniel said. "I know Edna isn't your favorite person, but I cared about her very much. There is a side to Edna that most people don't know. She longs to be loved, but love never seems to be enough, almost like she's searching for an amount of love that's not humanly possible."

"I know several people like that. They are restless by nature and try to fill the void in their lives with all kinds of things. The search doesn't end until they open their hearts to God's love," Charlotte said.

Daniel sighed into the phone. "I used to think it was you *Englisch* people who made things complicated. But I'm having to rethink that as I watch the situations around me unfolding."

Charlotte put the truck in park and took the key out of the ignition. "I will pray for all of you, Daniel, but is there anything specific I can pray for, for you?"

He was quiet for a few moments, then said, "*Ya*. I think that I'd like you to pray that I'm able to trust again too. But only after you've prayed for Annie and *mei mamm*. They both need extra prayers right now."

"Done. I'm going to pray for all good things for your family, and I'm going to pray that you and I both learn to trust again and that I will trust God as strongly as you do."

"That's a *gut* prayer, my *Englisch* friend."

Charlotte's heart warmed. "Are we friends now? I'm pretty sure you didn't like me too much a couple of weeks ago."

"I only knew you as Mary Troyer, the woman who pretended to be Amish and lied to Hannah and her family." He paused, and Charlotte realized she was holding her breath. "But now I see someone who puts the needs of others before her own. I know it must not have been easy taking care of Lena when she went to Houston for her cancer treatments. And you've been very *gut* to Annie and Jacob. So, *ya* . . . I hope we're friends now."

"Thank you for saying that. Jacob and Annie are sweet kids. They'll get things figured out."

A friend. Charlotte could use one of those. Hannah had been busy with wedding plans prior to this crisis with Jacob and Annie. But even before all this, Hannah rarely called. She missed having a close friend.

"I have a question. When things settle down with Jacob and Annie, will everyone pack up their cell phones and go back to the way things used to be, using the phones mostly for emergencies?"

Daniel laughed. "I don't know. Almost everyone has one, especially those who do business with the *Englisch*. I know some of the elders have never used cell phones, and they are against them. They are farmers who still have a phone shanty that several families share. The rule is, phones of any type are for emergencies only, but it's a rule that isn't enforced by the bishop."

Charlotte recalled a prior conversation. "Careful, you'll turn into us."

"And we can't have that." He laughed, but Charlotte grumbled.

"Ahhh, I left my sunglasses at your house. I knew something didn't feel right. I gotta go back. They were a gift from Lena, and I don't want her to think I carelessly lost them." She pulled Big Red back onto the road, grinding the gears as she got going.

A few minutes later, Charlotte bounded up the porch steps of the Byler residence two at a time.

"Forget something?" Annie was holding Charlotte's glasses when she answered the door.

"Yep." Charlotte put the glasses on. "Thanks." She turned to leave but saw Annie flinch. "What's wrong?" She pushed the sunglasses up on her head.

"My stomach is cramping." Annie came onto the porch and closed the screen door behind her. She bent over slightly and clutched her stomach.

Charlotte thought for a few moments. "When are you due?"

"Um . . ." Annie counted on her fingers. "July, I think."

Charlotte stared at her. "Annie, it's almost April. That would make you six months pregnant."

She nodded. "*Ya*, I know."

Charlotte scratched her head. "You don't look six months pregnant. Are you sure you're calculating correctly?"

"*Nee*, not for certain. But I think."

"Have you gained much weight?" Charlotte glanced at Annie's stomach, knowing Annie's baggy clothes could hide a growing tummy.

"I've gained a little." She cleared her throat. "But I would have thought I'd be feeling the baby moving by now."

Charlotte tried to keep her expression from registering shock and bit her bottom lip. She wasn't an expert on pregnancy, but the baby should be moving by now. "Are you bleeding at all?"

"Of course not." Annie frowned. "We might only go to school through the eighth grade, but girls know how this works. I haven't had a period in six months."

Charlotte took a deep breath in an effort to calm her fears. "I'm not really talking about a period. I was just wondering if you were spotting, you know . . . like having a few drops of blood occasionally." Charlotte remembered when a girl she used to work with started spotting in her second trimester and ended up losing the baby. But Annie shook her head.

"*Nee.* No blood. I, uh . . . have to go to the bathroom a lot, though."

Charlotte took a step closer to her. "Can I feel your stomach?"

Annie shrugged. "I guess. It's been crampy like this before, but then it goes away."

Charlotte laid a hand on Annie's middle. There was a small pooch, but nothing to indicate Annie was six months pregnant. She had to have miscalculated. "When was your last doctor's appointment?"

"I haven't been to the doctor. Jacob said you can't get pregnant from only one time. I didn't take the test for a while after we . . ." She frowned. "After we were bad."

Charlotte fought to keep the worry from her voice. "We need to get you checked out by a doctor."

Annie put both hands on her stomach and blinked, her bottom lip trembling. "Why? What do you think is wrong?"

Charlotte wasn't going to alarm Annie in case she was wrong. But she hadn't gained much weight, and if there was a baby, it wasn't moving. "I'm not saying anything is wrong. You took a pregnancy test, right?"

"*Ya*, one of those kinds you do at home. It said it's 99 percent accurate."

Charlotte went back to the truck and returned with

her phone. She googled clinics in the area and called the nearest one. Since Annie was listening, she just said, "I have a friend who is young and six months pregnant, but she hasn't been to a doctor. Can I bring her in today?"

The woman on the other end of the line said their schedule was full today, but asked if it was urgent. Charlotte glanced at Annie. "I'm not sure, maybe." She waited while the woman found a slot to squeeze Annie in, then once she'd hit End, Charlotte told Annie that her appointment was at three o'clock.

Twelve

Jacob pulled his suitcase out from under his bed and opened it. Then he shut it and put it back. His urge to run off was stronger than ever. He'd even taken his telescope out the night before, remembering how much he used to enjoy looking at the stars, then reading about the various constellations. But he was sick of reading about constellations and sick of reading about everything else out in the *Englisch* world that he wasn't able to see or do. Then he recalled his time in Texas and thought how it wasn't all that grand either.

"What is wrong with me, Lord?" His mind was messed up. He'd done wrong by Annie, first by getting her pregnant, and now by not wanting to be with her. What kind of a man had he turned into? Nothing was right in his head. It was hard to get out of bed some mornings. And he'd done something over the past week that he'd never done before. He'd bought some pills from an *Englisch* boy he knew. Pills that made you feel not so messed up. He'd taken two last night.

Jacob could already picture his parents dragging him by his ears to marry Annie. And Annie would marry him because her own father would insist on it. What if they really loved each other, but not the way you're supposed to if you're planning to get married? But after his last conversation with Annie, he wasn't sure the choice was his to make anymore.

He pulled his pants on and slipped on a maroon long-sleeved shirt to hide his tattoo, then he sat down on the edge of his bed and put his face in his hands. And for the second time in recent memory, he cried. The burden of his actions bore down on him so hard he could barely breathe.

Annie looked around the clinic, a small place with maybe a dozen people waiting to see a doctor. Charlotte sat next to her, but they'd barely spoken on their way here. Something was wrong. Annie could feel it, and Charlotte's somber expression and mood were apparent, even though Charlotte was obviously trying to hide her concern.

God is punishing me.

"Annie Byler."

Charlotte stood up when Annie did, and they walked toward a nurse dressed in blue pants and a blue shirt. She looked about the same age as Charlotte. The name on the woman's badge read Amelia. Annie could only recall one person she'd ever met with that name, and she hadn't been a very nice lady. This Amelia said hello, but with little enthusiasm.

After Amelia took Annie's blood pressure and temperature, she asked her to get on the scale. She'd gained seven pounds since she'd found out she was pregnant. That didn't seem like much to Annie. Then Annie had to give the nurse a urine sample.

They followed Amelia down a hallway. It smelled of ammonia and something else Annie didn't recognize. Amelia asked them to wait in a small room until the doctor came in.

She and Charlotte sat down in two chairs against the wall. Annie eyed the table in the middle of the room. It had a white paper covering, and hanging at the end, on both sides, were metal rings shaped like ovals. She knew that's where she'd have to put her feet for the doctor to examine her. She started to tremble, wondering if it was going to hurt. And worrying if her baby was okay. She wouldn't have reason to think this if Charlotte hadn't scared her.

"Will they tell me if it's a boy or a girl? Will they know that?"

"They might do an ultrasound," Charlotte said with

an insincere smile. "Then I guess it's up to you if you want to know the sex."

Annie cringed just hearing the word that had gotten her into this mess in the first place. *Please, God, let my baby be okay.* She felt crampy again.

About thirty minutes later, a doctor with gray hair and gold-framed glasses walked into the room and introduced himself as Dr. Newton.

Annie burst into tears.

~

Charlotte paced outside the room as a tearful Annie underwent her first ever vaginal exam. A few minutes later, Dr. Newton and Amelia came out of the room.

"Annie is getting dressed, then I'll let her fill you in on the details."

Charlotte couldn't stand it. "Is she okay?"

Dr. Newton nodded. "She seems to be just fine." He walked away before Charlotte could question him further. She waited a minute for Annie to get dressed, then tapped on the door.

"Come in."

Annie was sitting on the examining table fully dressed in her dark green smock and black apron. Her prayer covering was lopsided, but she had a broad smile on her face. "Thank goodness you're okay. The baby is okay too?"

Annie jumped off the table, bounced on her toes,

and locked eyes with Charlotte, still grinning. "I'm not pregnant."

Charlotte just stood there. "Huh?"

"The doctor said that sometimes a pregnancy test will show that you're pregnant, but you're really not. He said I might have done the test wrong, but I don't think I did. The cup I used could have been contaminated, like by soap or detergent. Or if the pregnancy test had expired, it might have shown a positive sign. But whatever it was, I'm not going to have a baby."

"But you gained weight, and you missed your periods. What did the doctor say about that?"

Annie shrugged. "I only gained seven pounds." She tapped a finger to her chin. "Probably from all the cupcakes I ate when I first thought I was pregnant. I couldn't get enough of them. I gave myself permission to eat anything I wanted. And the doctor said my missed periods could be stress." She lifted up on her toes again. "Either way, he said I am not pregnant. They did a test with my urine, and it came out negative, and they did an ultrasound. They took my blood too. They'll call me in twenty-four hours with the results from that, but he's sure I'm not pregnant." She raised the sleeve of her dress to show Charlotte a cotton ball held with tape. "He wants me to follow up with my regular doctor about my missed periods. I've missed my monthlies before, but never six months in a row. But there is no baby."

"Wow." This was a much better prognosis than

Charlotte could have imagined, but as she recalled all of the drama, she wondered how things had gotten to this point. *Everything happens for a reason.* She let that thought soak in for a minute.

On the way home, Annie called Daniel and filled him in on the news from her doctor visit. It was a brief call, and she said they'd arrive home shortly. She asked her brother to tell Jacob. She wasn't ready to talk to him just yet.

~

Daniel found his parents after Annie called, and when he told them Annie wasn't pregnant, it was as if the clouds had parted and rained mixed blessings down on them. His mother cried, which she did a lot these days, and Daniel honestly couldn't tell if she was happy or sad. But his father's smile filled his face. It was quickly replaced by a scowl.

"Annie will not see that boy." His father looped his thumbs beneath his suspenders, then grunted.

Daniel wasn't sure Annie wanted to be with Jacob, but one thing he knew for certain—tell a seventeen-year-old they can't do something, and that's all they'll want to do. But now was not the time to push the issue. "Annie asked me to tell Jacob, and I think it's best to do it in person. She doesn't want to see him right now."

"*Ya, ya*," his mother said as she dabbed at her eyes with the corner of her apron.

Daniel found Jacob at his house, in the driveway washing down the buggies. Jacob turned off the water when Daniel stepped out of the buggy.

"What's wrong? Is it Annie? The baby?" Jacob asked as he met up with Daniel in the yard.

"Annie is fine. She went to the doctor, and she's okay. And Jacob . . ." Daniel paused, unsure how Jacob was going to react. "There is no baby. There never was. Annie isn't pregnant."

Jacob's mouth fell open as jumbled thoughts appeared to assault his senses. A glazed look fell over his face, and Daniel noticed that his eyes were glassy, as though he'd been sleeping, not washing the buggies on a sunny afternoon.

"You okay?" Daniel asked as he stroked the stubble on his chin, eyeing the boy.

"*Ya, ya.*" Jacob took off his straw hat and ran a hand through his blond hair. "I guess this is *gut* news."

Daniel recalled everyone saying a baby was a blessing, but he felt relief in this news, especially for Annie and Jacob, who surely didn't seem ready to be parents. Neither of them knew what they wanted. He waited for Jacob to absorb this news as the boy put his hat back on, his eyes still unfocused and red. Jacob had probably had his share of sleepless nights, like Annie, but this looked like something more than lack of sleep.

"Jacob . . ." Daniel waited for Jacob to look at him. "Our father feels strongly you and Annie need some time apart." He waited to let that soak in. "And Annie doesn't want to see or talk to you right now."

Jacob nodded just before Daniel turned back to his buggy.

Charlotte kissed the envelope that held her check, the big one she'd been waiting for. Then she closed her laptop and set it on the foot of the bed. She'd just finished a big editing project—and much faster than she normally would have back home. She could give Ryan credit for that since she wasn't wasting her time worrying that he was cheating on her. It had become a fact. Plus, there were a lot fewer distractions living without electricity.

She could hear faint giggling from the porch downstairs. Hannah and Isaac. Hopefully, now that Jacob and Annie were home, life could get back to normal for all of them, except for their non-Amish friend who was staying with them for a while.

Charlotte stretched out her legs and crossed her ankles in the dimly lit room. As she lay her head against her pillow, she thought about Ethan. What would it be like if he were alive now? Chances were good that Charlotte would have continued her old way of thinking—that the Amish were some sort of cult—so she wouldn't have come for a visit last year and never would have understood why Ethan chose to live here. She wouldn't have met Hannah and her family. Every single thing that had happened in her life had led her to this exact moment in time, all according to God's perfect plan. And maybe if she said that over and over in her head, she'd understand what God's perfect plan was for her. Or maybe she wasn't supposed to know.

She missed Buddy, who was still choosing the foot of Amos's bed and not hers. She didn't get too far into that thought when her phone rang.

"Is it too late to be calling?" Daniel asked when she answered.

"No, it's fine. I just finished working, and Hannah is downstairs with Isaac. How did your parents take the news that Annie isn't pregnant?"

"I know *Daed* was happy to hear it. I'm not sure about *Mamm*. I think she might have gotten used to the idea of being a grandmother."

"It's probably normal to have mixed emotions. Although Annie didn't seem to have any. She was elated by the news. What about Jacob? What did he have to say?"

"Uh, well . . ." Daniel exhaled. "He was happy, I think. But the boy didn't look normal to me. His eyes were red and bloodshot, a little glazed over."

"He's probably tired and worried about all this."

Daniel was quiet for a few moments. "He looked drunk."

Charlotte sat taller against her pillow. She'd never seen alcohol at the King house. But she recalled the dazed, drunken look her mother used to get after Charlotte's dad had knocked her around. And Mom had gotten the same look after Dad had gone to prison—then it was her mother who started knocking Charlotte and Ethan around. But there was always more than booze involved. If her parents could be credited with anything, it would be that Charlotte didn't abuse alcohol or drugs, and to her knowledge, Ethan hadn't either. They'd seen the effects of addiction much too young. *Face your demons, Charlotte*, she could hear her therapist saying. *No thank you.*

"Do you think Jacob takes drugs? Like recreationally?" That seemed unlikely in an Amish community, but maybe she was naive to think that.

"*Nee*, we have our problems like everyone else. But if our teens are doing drugs, I've never heard anything about it."

Charlotte was aware that she was overly fearful about suicide. Every time she heard someone was depressed, she wanted to jump in and save them. But she had to believe that Jacob was just tired and stressed. "Maybe things will settle down for all of you now."

"I'm going to have to trust that Annie and Jacob will make the right choices."

Charlotte smiled again, warmed by Daniel's evident love of his sister.

"I wanted to let you know that I got your plumbing all fixed."

"Thank you so much for doing that."

"And how much was Annie's doctor's visit? She said

you paid for it, but she couldn't remember how much it was. I'll pay you back—just let me know the amount."

Charlotte wasn't going to mention the money, but it was nice of Daniel to offer to reimburse her. "Consider it payment for the plumbing work."

"*Nee, nee.* You bought the parts, so I'm not out anything but a little time."

They chatted for a few more minutes, but when Daniel thanked her again for taking good care of Annie, there was an air of finality in his voice that left Charlotte feeling . . . sad.

"Well, I've enjoyed getting to know you a little bit," she said. "I love it here, but I couldn't stand it if everyone still saw me as Mary Troyer. She's gone forever, replaced by Charlotte Dolinsky—what you see is what you get."

Daniel chuckled. "I like Charlotte a lot better than Mary anyway."

Annie pried her ear from Daniel's door. She hadn't meant to eavesdrop, but on her way back from the bathroom, she'd heard her name, so she'd stopped outside his bedroom door. Her own love life might be in shambles, but she was happy to hear Charlotte and Daniel getting to know each other. She wanted more than anything for Daniel to be happy. Annie hadn't cared all that much for Edna, as she'd broken Daniel's heart. And she didn't seem to be genuine when she spoke. Charlotte had proven herself to be a good person. *But Charlotte isn't Amish.* Maybe they'd both be better off just staying friends. But then she thought about how Ethan had joined the Amish for Hannah. *It happens.*

She lay down on her bed and put a hand across her empty stomach. Life would be easier now that she and Jacob would be able to make decisions for themselves without another life to consider. But she'd gotten used to the idea of having a baby, so she felt an emptiness despite her relief. She couldn't sleep, so she turned up the lantern. She thought about Jacob. Was he happy she wasn't pregnant? Would he still want to get married? Did she? She wondered what he was doing right now.

Jacob latched onto the handrail as he fought his way down the stairs, his socked feet threatening to slide out from under him. He was almost to the landing when he heard footsteps behind him. When he glanced over his shoulder, it was just enough to throw him off balance, and he landed on his behind with a thud. He looked up to see Hannah in her robe and bare feet offering him a hand. He accepted and moaned as he stood up.

"What are you doing?" Hannah let go of him and thrust her hands on her hips. "It's one in the morning."

"I'm getting a glass of water. Someone moved the

glass that was in our bathroom." He sneered at her. "What are you doing up?"

She leaned closer to him and sniffed. Jacob backed up a little but had to catch himself before he stumbled.

"Have you been drinking alcohol?"

"*Nee*," he said in a whisper, frowning.

"I heard you banging into the walls going down the hallway to get to the stairs, like you're a drunkard."

"I didn't want to take a chance of waking you or Charlotte by bringing the lantern."

"*Ach*, well . . . this is better. You falling down the stairs. You'd better hope we don't wake up Charlotte's dog. He'll go nuts and wake up everyone." Hannah pulled a flashlight from the robe in her pocket and shined it in front of them as they went down the last couple of stairs and crossed the living room to the kitchen. "Charlotte told me that Daniel said you acted weird when he told you about Annie not being pregnant."

Jacob rolled his eyes and grunted. "Wouldn't you have acted weird? I'd just found out that I wasn't going to be a father."

Hannah shone the flashlight in his face, enough that he had to put up a hand to block the light. "Quit it."

"Daniel said your eyes were glassy like you were a drunkard."

"Put the light down, and quit saying the word *drunkard*. I'm not drunk."

"Your eyes look all glassy and strange right now."

Jacob found a glass and filled it with water. "So do yours. I just woke up."

Hannah didn't say anything and followed Jacob back to the stairs. "Something's not right with you," she said once they got in the upstairs hallway.

"Leave me alone, Hannah."

Jacob closed the door to his bedroom. He couldn't deal with her right now in addition to everything else going on in his head. The two pills he'd taken didn't seem to be working as well. He found the bottle of Xanax he'd bought from the *Englisch* kid and took a third one. Within a few minutes, he could feel the demons leaving his mind like little fish jumping from a fishbowl, making him breathless at first, followed by calm. Peacefulness found the way to Jacob's mind. Then sleep came.

Thirteen

Charlotte carried all her electronics into the coffee shop and started charging everything while she waited for Annie. Her young friend had asked if Charlotte wanted to meet her for coffee this morning, which worked out well since Charlotte's laptop and phone were almost out of juice. She'd overheard bits and pieces of conversations between Lena, Amos, and Hannah that suggested things were getting back to normal. And Charlotte had been glad to hear that Annie's father had welcomed her back with open arms.

Charlotte thought about the only father figure she'd known, aside from God the Father, and that was Amos. She was still disappointed that they hadn't talked about everything that happened last year. Several times Charlotte had wanted to pin him down, tell him again how sorry she was for lying to them. But she'd told him that, and he'd walked away. Charlotte had asked Hannah about it again, even after both Lena and Hannah said Amos had forgiven her. Hannah told Charlotte that it was hard for her father to show emotion. Charlotte wasn't sure if that was completely true or if Hannah was trying to spare Charlotte's feelings.

Annie walked into the coffee shop a few minutes later, cozied up to Charlotte, and snuck her a cell phone. "Can you charge mine too?" she whispered.

Charlotte smiled, nodding.

Once they both had a warm beverage in front of them at a small table in the back, Annie grinned. "I heard Daniel on the phone with you Saturday night. I was on my way to the bathroom."

Charlotte raised an eyebrow. "Annie Byler, were you eavesdropping on your brother?"

"Daniel is the most wonderful man." Annie reached over and touched Charlotte's hand. It was a sweet gesture, but Charlotte wondered where Annie was going with this.

"Yes, Daniel seems like a good guy, and he certainly loves you to the moon and back." Charlotte blew on her steaming coffee.

Annie eyed Charlotte. "Where are you going to live after your little blue house sells?"

Charlotte shrugged. "I don't know. I've made some huge changes lately, so I'm just taking things one day at a time. And no one's knocking down my door to buy the house. Since it doesn't have electricity, it would have to be someone who is Amish or a person willing to have it wired for power. It had a plumbing problem, but Daniel repaired that for me."

Annie smiled. "He's like that . . . Daniel. Always doing for others."

Charlotte tucked her hair behind her ears, then took another sip of coffee. "He told me he had a bad breakup awhile back, but I'm sure he will find a nice woman to share his life with."

Annie sighed. "Edna wasn't right for him." But then her face lit up. "You two must be getting close if you are talking about such personal things."

"Not really." Charlotte felt the conversation shifting to a place she wasn't comfortable with. "So, what is going on with you and Jacob?"

Annie put her elbows on the table, then rested her chin on her hands. "I don't know. I guess you could say we are taking things one day at a time too." She paused. "Do you miss your ex-boyfriend, Ryan?"

Charlotte considered lying, but only briefly. "Yes, sometimes I do. Even though he cheated on me and made me feel like a crazy person for checking his text messages—yes, I miss him. Actually, I think I miss what I thought we had more than anything."

"I would miss Jacob, too, if he was out of my life completely." Annie fidgeted with a napkin. "Daniel talks about you a lot."

"What?" Charlotte sat taller. "Why?"

"I don't know. You tell me." Annie grinned. "Do you think Daniel is handsome?"

Incredibly. "Uh, yeah, he is a nice-looking man."

Annie eyed her critically. "Life is short, Charlotte. And you're not getting any younger."

Charlotte half laughed, half snorted, almost blowing coffee out her nose. She assumed Annie was trying to be funny. But Annie's lips were flat, and Charlotte realized that in Annie's mind, Charlotte was practically ready for retirement.

"Sweetie, I see where you are going with this, but your brother and I live very different lives."

Annie beamed. "Opposites attract."

Charlotte shook her head. "It's never going to happen." She was surprised that Annie was even suggesting it since Charlotte wasn't Amish, and that wasn't going to change. Unlike her young friends, Charlotte had no intention of being haphazard with her love life anymore.

Annie smiled broadly. "Never say never."

A couple of days later another check arrived. Charlotte was beginning to relax about her work status because this new living situation allowed her to be more productive than she'd ever been. She was seeing less and less of Hannah, and even though she missed their late-night chats at bedtime, it warmed her heart to hear soft voices and laughter out on the porch. She knew Hannah and Isaac were finalizing their wedding plans for the fall.

She closed her laptop and lowered the flame on the lantern, content to snuggle down into her pillow and talk to God a little before she fell asleep.

She jumped when her cell phone vibrated on the nightstand. Even though she'd deleted his contact information, she recognized Ryan's number. She stared at the phone for a few seconds before answering it.

"I just wanted to check on you," Ryan said with a tenderness and familiarity that caused Charlotte's eyes to tear up.

"It's not your job to check up on me anymore."

He breathed heavily into the phone. "I messed up so badly, Charlotte. I—I miss you. I hate myself for what I did to you, to us."

His voice cracked as he spoke, and a tear slipped down her cheek. She was thankful Ryan couldn't see the effect he still had on her.

"Is there any chance . . . any chance of you coming back? Could we even try to put things back together again?"

Oh, Ryan. How many times did I ask you that same question? She fought to keep her voice steady. "I don't think so. I'm starting over here in Lancaster County."

There was silence on the other end of the line. "I want all good things for you, Charlotte," he said softly. "Are you back in counseling?"

This hit a nerve. "No."

"I think it was really helping you."

His voice had gone flat, and Charlotte trembled. "Why do you do that?"

"Do what?"

"You bring up counseling like I'm the one with all the issues. Apparently you have some issues as well, including the inability to be faithful."

"I told you I was sorry." His words were void of the kindness he'd shown seconds earlier.

Charlotte clenched her fists, seething. He could pour on the charm when he wanted something, but once she'd made it clear that they couldn't work things out, he tried to make her feel bad about herself again. Charlotte felt bad enough about herself for the both of them.

"Anyway," he said after a pause, "I really thought you'd want to give it another go, but I guess I was wrong."

"So, did Shelley dump you?" She spat the words at him.

"Charlotte, I'll just let you go. I can see that you haven't changed. Get yourself back into counseling." And he hung up.

She raised the phone high above her head, tempted to send it crashing into the wall, but instead she dropped it in her lap and cried. A minute later, it rang again.

Daniel. She stared at the phone and then slowly set it on her nightstand. Did Annie go back home and put ideas in Daniel's head, the way she'd tried to do with Charlotte? When he left a voice mail, she listened to it.

"*Wie bischt*, Charlotte. I need to talk to you. Can you please call me back? I'll leave *mei* phone on."

Charlotte didn't want to do anything to lead Daniel on.

She slid under the covers, shut her eyes, and prayed for sleep.

~

Jacob flushed the entire bottle of pills down the commode, deciding that no matter how confused and messed up he felt, the pills just seemed to make things worse. For starters, both Daniel and Hannah had thought he was drunk, and Jacob had never been one to drink, not even on the few occasions when he'd had an opportunity to do so with his buddies during their *rumschpringe*. Besides, he'd spent the past couple of days meeting Annie in the late afternoon to talk, which seemed easier now that they weren't under so much pressure.

They'd opted for the coffee shop today. Annie was there when Jacob walked in, and he found her toward the back at a table for two, sipping on what he presumed was one of the frozen coffees she liked. She already had a cup of black coffee waiting for him along with a whoopie pie for each of them.

"*Wie bischt*," he said as he slid into the seat across from her. "Did you make a decision?"

Annie finished taking a sip from her cup, then nodded. "Everyone keeps asking what you and I are going to do, if we're going to get married, date, or break up. Even *mei daed* asked, and I honestly think he's hoping we break up."

Jacob frowned. "What do *you* want, Annie?"

Annie folded her hands on top of the table. "I've already been baptized. I made my decision to live here and raise a family here already." Her expression brightened a little. "Even though I did enjoy listening to some of Aunt Faye's music and having the heater on at night. Of course, Aunt Faye's cooking offset those things."

Jacob's adrenaline spiked at the thought that Annie might accept his offer.

Annie's eyes softened and her expression fell. "But there's not much about the *Englisch* world that interests me, Jacob. I'm not going to give up my life here to go on a whimsical journey with you while you decide whether or not you want a life here or outside of our community. You've already tried that. And you were willing to leave me to seek out happiness for yourself."

"But I came back."

"*Ya*, and now you are ready to leave again."

"With you, Annie! I want us to go together."

"You have an itch that you apparently didn't scratch during your time in Texas, because here you are again, feeling like a caged animal." She paused as a scowl emerged. "And you want me to give up my life, without us even being married, to travel with you on this journey without a destination. I can't do that."

"Annie, do you love me?" Jacob held his breath.

She opened her mouth but nothing came out, and Jacob felt a stab of panic, still unsure what he wanted but not prepared to lose Annie altogether.

"I do love you," she finally said, with barely the hint of a smile on her face. "But I don't know if my love will ever be enough for you."

Jacob stared at his coffee getting cold, then locked eyes with her. "Well, how will we know if we don't try?"

Annie's eyes widened as she pressed her lips into a thin smile. "Do you ever think before you speak? Do you hear what you're saying? 'Gee, Annie, I love you, but I don't know if it's enough, but please leave your life without being married to me, and let's travel into the *Englisch* world to see if I can love you enough to want to make you my priority?'"

Jacob hunched his shoulders and cringed as her voice raised enough for the few patrons in the coffee shop to hear loud and clear. He was speechless, but clearly Annie was not.

"So, Jacob, you do whatever it is that you need to do. Leave!" She flew her hands toward him like she was shooing away a bug. "Just go. Figure out your life. But don't expect me to sit around waiting for you. For such a book-smart man, you don't have a shred of common sense when it comes to relationships." She stood and picked up her coffee.

"Um . . . are we breaking up, then?" Jacob stayed in his seat.

Annie leaned toward him, close to his ear. "*Ya*, Jacob. We are breaking up."

Jacob sat there for the next thirty minutes sipping his cold coffee and thinking he should feel worse than he did and knowing that he would plan better before he left again.

Daniel gave Charlotte until Saturday evening to return his call, but when she hadn't, he dialed her number.

"*Wie bischt*," he said after she answered. "It's Daniel."

"Oh, hey. Sorry I didn't return your call the other day."

He waited for her to offer an explanation, but when she didn't, he thought he heard her eating. "Did I call you at a bad time?"

"Not really. I'm sitting on my bed eating strawberry shortcake ice cream. I might eat the entire half gallon."

"Um . . . is there a reason for this ice cream binge? I heard once that girls do that when they're upset."

"Yep. It's true. And I guess I'm upset a lot, because I seem to eat a lot of ice cream." Her words were clipped, her tone sarcastic.

"Do you want to tell me what's wrong? Have I said or done something to upset you?"

She breathed into the phone like she was blowing up a balloon, long and heavy. "Noooo . . . you didn't do anything. Ryan called a few days ago, and it's just left me feeling like a failure, at relationships and my life in general."

Daniel could relate, but he wasn't sure what to say.

"Ryan might have helped me find my way to God, but his actions don't indicate that he is practicing what he preaches. That is as disappointing to me as the breakup." She drew in a breath. "But it's over. And I'm not going to let him make me feel like a nutcase, which is exactly what I've let him do since Wednesday."

Daniel scratched his head, still unsure what to say. "How many gallons of ice cream do you think it will take before you feel better?"

"I'm gonna need at least one more gallon of strawberry shortcake to complete the healing process. Possibly more."

Daniel grinned, picturing her shoveling ice cream into her mouth. But then he remembered why he'd originally called. "Listen, I need to tell you something. No cause for alarm, but I stopped by your house the other day, and once again the door was unlocked. Has your real estate agent shown it this week?"

"I talked to Yvonne earlier today. There haven't been any showings. And the price is really low, so I'm disappointed about that, but it wouldn't be anyone at her office leaving the door open . . . That's weird."

"Maybe someone is spending the night there."

"What? Who would do that, and how would they get in?"

"I don't know. I checked all the windows to make sure they were still locked, and they were. But a package of toilet paper was sitting on the bathroom counter. I don't remember seeing it before."

"I'm sure someone at the real estate office must have put it in there. That doesn't mean someone is staying there."

"When I was checking all the windows, I found a bag of trash out back. It's been there awhile, but an animal had ripped it open. It was mostly stuff Isaac used to work on the house, empty tubes of caulk, wads of painting tape . . . stuff like that. But I think what drew the cats or dogs to the garbage was food. Chicken bones were strewn everywhere. And before you say that Isaac probably ate chicken while he was working on the house, there was a box from the chicken place up the road on Lincoln Highway. The receipt was stapled to the box, dated that same day."

"So you think a homeless person is camping out in my house at night?" She laughed. "And using the bathroom and eating chicken."

"Maybe, I don't know." He shrugged, fighting a yawn. "Whoever is going in and out keeps leaving the door unlocked, a sure giveaway that someone's been there. If they have a key to get in, they should have a key to get out. *Ach*, I hauled all the trash away."

"Thank you for doing that," Charlotte said around a bite of ice cream. "I will call Yvonne to make sure no one at her office has any reason to be going in or out. Maybe kids are finding a way in, teenagers."

"Maybe. You said Edna and Ethan carried on for a while. Maybe Edna has a key. Although I can't imagine why she'd be going in and out."

"Do you feel comfortable asking Edna about it, if maybe she has a key for some reason?"

Not really. "I—I can." Daniel recalled his last encounter with Edna out in the barn. After the way she'd come on to Daniel, it occurred to him that maybe Edna was the one going in and out, maybe meeting another man there. But that seemed like a stretch.

"If you're not comfortable—"

"*Nee*, it's okay. I'll talk to her. She has a booth at the farmers' market two days a week. I can find her there. I doubt it's her, but at least we can rule it out."

"Okay. I'll ask Hannah to check with Isaac, too, in case he had some reason to go in there. As far as I know, Isaac still has a key. If we both come up dry, I'll just have to have the locks changed."

It took Daniel a few moments to connect the phrase "come up dry" with what they were talking about. "*Ya*, okay. It's a nice house. I'm sure it will sell soon."

"Actually, I entertained the idea of keeping it, maybe renting it out or keeping it as a vacation place before I decided to move here. That might sound weird since that's where Ethan died, but I feel a sense of Ethan inside the house—not in a creepy way or anything. The only thing that bothers me is that tree."

Daniel knew which tree she meant.

"I hate that tree," she said softly. "But I like the house and the location. It was Ethan's last home, and it's really all I have left of him. Hannah has a few things in storage that were Ethan's, but otherwise . . ."

He should let her get some sleep. Or finish stuffing herself with ice cream until she felt better.

"I had Isaac paint all the walls white, beadboard and all. But if I were keeping it, I'd leave the beadboard that goes halfway up the walls white, then paint soft, light colors in the other rooms. I'd keep that claw-foot tub too. But I need to sell it, so hopefully the right person will come along. Probably Amish since there isn't any electricity. Either way, I prayed for peace and happiness to whoever ends up in the house."

Daniel told her they probably both needed to get some sleep, and she agreed. He didn't want to worry her about the other things he'd found in that trash bag. It was enough for her to know that he believed someone was staying in the house at night.

Fourteen

Jacob sat with his mother, father, and Hannah around the kitchen table after breakfast Monday morning. It was pouring rain outside, so no one was in a hurry to do much of anything, although his mother would tend to her goats soon, no matter the weather. Charlotte had gone upstairs after breakfast and said she needed to work. Jacob cleared his throat, deciding there was never going to be a good time to tell them his plans.

His father lifted his eyes above the copy of *die Botschaft* he was reading and peered at Jacob through his reading glasses. Jacob's mother and Hannah were making out a grocery list and didn't look his way until he cleared his throat again.

"I have something to talk to you all about," he said once he had their full attention, his foot tapping under the table like it had a mind of its own. Charlotte's dog had finally stopped barking at him, but Buddy was never far from *Daed*, sharing space near Jacob's foot under the table. He drew in a deep breath, trying to prepare himself for the backlash that was sure to come. "I sold my telescope for almost as much money as I paid for it."

His father lowered the newspaper and glanced at his mother before turning back to Jacob. "Why?"

Daed, *always a man of few words*, Jacob thought as he tried to recall the speech he'd planned.

Hannah leaned back in her chair and huffed. "Because he needs the money to leave." She glared at Jacob, then almost hissed as she went on. "He's leaving us . . . again."

"Is this true, Jacob?" *Daed* stroked the length of his beard, frowning.

Jacob nodded, then looked at Hannah. "Annie doesn't want to be with me."

His sister pointed a finger at him. "She used to. She wanted to marry you. But I'm sure Annie doesn't want to leave here, and she knows you do. You're making a mistake, Jacob!"

"You can't tell me that, Hannah. I'm not baptized. This is my *rumschpringe*, and I have a right to live my life however I see fit. That's why we have a running-around period, remember?" Jacob's voice grew louder. This was hard enough without having Hannah spew ugliness in his direction. "It's not your choice!"

Hannah's face turned red and her eyes watered. "You don't know what you want, and I don't understand why you think you need to leave." She tossed her hands up. "You already did leave, but you came back."

"I thought . . . I thought Annie was with child, and things were confusing. I owe it to myself to try again." Jacob wouldn't be shunned by the bishop since he wasn't baptized, but his family could still choose their own form of shunning. As much as he feared that, to stay would be too much to bear.

Hannah opened her mouth to talk, but their father beat her to it.

"Your *bruder* is right. This is his time to decide how he will live his life. You don't have to agree with his choices, but they are his to make." *Daed* looked at Jacob. "But you will do things differently this time. You will not sneak off in the middle of the night, nor will you be out of communication with your mother, keeping her worried all the time."

"But *Daed*, Jacob is choosing a life away from us, a life with the *Englisch*, and—"

Hannah stopped when their father held up a palm.

"Hannah, have you always chosen correctly?" *Daed* took off his glasses and set them on the table. "We all loved Ethan, and I say this not to hurt you but to make you understand. We had our doubts about Ethan, an *Englisch* man coming into our district, courting our daughter, and . . ." He trailed off when Hannah's eyes started to fill with tears again.

"But *Daed*, I didn't know Ethan would be unfaithful

to me. I didn't know he suffered from such a deep depression that he would take his own life. I just knew that I loved him." She swiped at her eyes. "How can you compare my situation to Jacob's? I never threatened to leave, not once."

Jacob stayed quiet, his chin on his chest. The last thing he ever wanted to do was to hurt his family or Annie. He reached up and rubbed his pounding temples, wishing he hadn't thrown the pills away, wishing he could just be happy marrying Annie and staying here.

Daed gazed into Hannah's eyes. "You are with the man you are meant to be with—Isaac. What I'm saying is that a wrong choice as viewed in the eyes of others might be exactly the choice necessary to set you on the path God has intended for you all along."

Now both of Jacob's socked feet were tapping against the wood floors. Buddy growled a little but then left the kitchen. Jacob wrung his clammy hands together in his lap. This was the most he'd heard from his father in a while. His dad was the last person Jacob could have predicted would come to his defense. He glanced at his mother, who had remained quiet with her head down.

"If Annie had truly been with child, it would have been his duty to marry her, to be a good husband and father. His actions would have cost him his right to choose." *Daed* stroked his beard. "I've spent much time thinking on this. We've all known Jacob isn't happy. And I believe we know that he didn't stay in the *Englisch* world long enough to know what he wanted, but he was prepared to come back and marry Annie, to do the right thing. Let the boy go."

Jacob couldn't stand it anymore. "*Mamm?*"

His mother slowly lifted her head and looked at him. Going along with one's husband was expected from an Amish *fraa*. For the most part, *Mamm* had allowed *Daed* to make final decisions, unless it was something big like this. *Daed* couldn't stand to see her hurting. If she put her foot down right now and said it would break her heart for Jacob to leave, *Daed* would let her override him, and Jacob would be back to where he'd been before, feeling the need to sneak out.

All eyes were on *Mamm*. The clock on the mantel in the living room ticked in slow rhythm, each second sounding louder than the last. Hannah's sniffling echoed in the quiet room as they all waited. Finally, his mother took a deep breath and exhaled it slowly.

"How much money did you get for your telescope?" She kept her gaze fixed on Jacob, no expression on her face.

"Nine hundred and eighty-two dollars." He recalled saving the money for over a year, and how his mother had not wanted him to make the purchase. It was his *daed* who had said it was Jacob's choice to make. But that was a telescope. This could be the rest of his life. "I—I know that won't last long, but I have a little money saved too. I'll get a job right away."

"Where will you go?" Hannah said with enough emotion on her face for all of them. "To Houston again?"

Jacob shook his head. "*Nee.* I'm not going back there. I want a fresh start, alone, so I can figure things out."

"Maybe you can stay near here? Maybe in the city of Lancaster? Or at least somewhere in Pennsylvania. You don't have to go far to figure things out." Hannah had taken over the conversation again, but Jacob was still waiting on his mother to say what was on her mind. Despite his jumbled thoughts, his father's approval, and Hannah's tears, if his mother begged him to stay, he would. She'd been through a lot, and for once—for her—he would put his selfish thoughts away. Jacob hadn't walked into the room feeling this way. He'd been defiant, ready to take them on in his moment of need. But as his mother looked at him, Jacob was sure she could see his soul, his heart talking to hers, begging for her blessing. *It'll kill me if I stay here,* Mamm.

His mother's chair scratched against the floor as she eased it backward and stood up. She went to the refrigerator and felt around on top of it, stretching and reaching until she pulled down an envelope and handed it to Jacob.

"This should be enough to help you get on your feet." She blinked her eyes a few times, then almost smiled. "*Sohn*, your father and I have always feared this day would come. Although, when you proposed to Annie, we thought you'd chosen to stay. Then when we thought

Annie was pregnant, I felt like you'd do the right thing in the end. But I fear it will always come back to this, to you wanting to leave."

I love you, Mamm.

His mother nodded as if Jacob had spoken the words aloud. "Stay in God's light, Jacob. Find peace." Then she turned and left the room. His father stood and followed behind her. Seconds later Hannah left too.

He was victorious. He should want to celebrate.

But he'd never felt more alone.

Daniel got off work early Tuesday afternoon. Erecting storage sheds provided a nice income, but it was laborious and he was happy to rest his muscles for an afternoon. He decided to go see Edna at home. She and John weren't at worship service Sunday or he would have talked to her then. Someone said John was down with a stomach bug. He would have preferred to find Edna on one of her days at the market selling jams and jellies, but Charlotte was anxious to know if Edna was going in and out of Ethan's house, whether she had a key or not. Edna loved to bake for others even though she was diabetic, which might explain the needles Daniel had found in the trash. But the syringes looked too big to belong to Edna. The more he thought about it, he was sure they couldn't be hers. He'd seen Edna give herself plenty of shots.

As he guided his buggy toward Edna's house, he had time to think about his conversations with Charlotte the past two days. Their phone calls had become more personal, and there was a playfulness between them that he enjoyed. They'd also spent time together after worship service on Sunday, but he wasn't sure their growing friendship was healthy for either one of them. Charlotte wasn't Amish. But he could see why Hannah and her family had grown to love her.

He pulled up to Edna's house, knowing her husband wouldn't be home yet and praying that Edna would behave herself. Sloshing through the soaked grass from the rains earlier, he made his way to the front door and knocked. Edna opened the door right away, and a smile stretched across her face.

"Daniel. What a nice surprise. Come in." She stepped aside, but he hesitated and looked toward the porch swing.

"Can we just sit outside? I like the smell of the rain, and it feels good out here."

"*Ya*, okay."

They both sat down on the swing, too close for Daniel's comfort, but better than their being alone inside. He took off his hat and turned slightly to face her. "I need to ask you something."

Edna's lips turned up at the corners and her eyes twinkled. "Okay."

She smelled good, like lavender, and it reminded Daniel of all the times he'd kissed her, thinking they had a future together. "Is there any reason why you might be going in and out of Ethan's old house?"

Edna's smile faded. She avoided his eyes and fingered the string on her *kapp*. "*Nee*, of course not. Why are you asking me this?"

"Someone's been going in and out, and Ethan's sister thought you might have a key." Daniel kept his eyes on Edna's, wanting to take note of every reaction now that her relationship with Ethan was out in the open.

Without looking up, she said, "I suppose that woman has been spewing lies about me."

Daniel stared at her. He'd cared about her so much at one point, but the thought of her seeing Ethan behind John's back turned his stomach. Granted, Edna hadn't married John yet, but it was still wrong. Then he thought about the way she'd come on to him recently, as a married woman. But he wasn't here to judge Edna, simply to make sure she hadn't recently been in the house. "Do you have a key to Ethan's house?"

Her eyes darted to his. "*Nee*. I do not. Why would I?"

Daniel considered telling her that half of their community knew about her having a relationship with Ethan while she was dating John, but there wasn't any point in that. "Someone has been going into the house. His sister—Charlotte—owns it, you know, and we are just trying to figure out who might be going in and out. All the doors and windows are locked. Charlotte asked me if I thought you might have a key."

"Charlotte is an evil woman. You can't believe anything she says. She lied to Hannah and the entire King family."

"The Kings think of Charlotte as family now. She took care of Lena when she was having treatments for her cancer in Houston. And we've had a bit of trouble with Annie and Jacob lately too. Charlotte was helpful with all of that as well. She's a *gut* person who regrets the lies she told us." His need to defend Charlotte was strong, and he wanted to say more, but Edna's bottom lip was twitching and her eyes blazed with anger.

"I cannot believe you would defend her."

Daniel reminded himself why he was here, and it wasn't to get into an argument with Edna. "Someone has been going in and out of the house, and I told her I would ask you. You said you don't have a key, so that's the end of it." Daniel stood up. "Sorry to have bothered you."

Edna wrapped the string of her *kapp* so tightly around her finger, the tip of her finger turned red. "I have no reason to go there. Don't listen to any of her rubbish, Daniel."

Stuffing his desire to respond, he instead said, "Have a good day, Edna. I'll let Charlotte know you don't have a key and that you haven't been in the *haus*."

She stood up and finally unwound the string from her finger. "You sound like you are friendly with that *Englisch* woman."

"I told you, we had some things going on with Annie and Jacob, and she helped us with that."

"I don't understand how an outsider could have helped."

"It's a long story, Edna, but Charlotte and I have become friends."

"Just beware of her, Daniel. She doesn't tell the truth. What kind of person pretends to be Amish, deceiving our entire community?"

He turned to her after taking a deep, calming breath. "Someone who loved her brother very much and wanted desperately to know why he killed himself. She'd lost her way for a while, but she stretches herself thin these days trying to do *gut* for others. Charlotte is strong in her faith, and we both know that the Lord forgives us the moment we ask Him to. Did you ask for forgiveness, Edna?" It just slipped out, and Daniel wished right away that he hadn't said it.

"I knew that woman was spreading lies about me. And you sound like you're in love with her! But I know that can't be true." She took a slow step toward him and cupped his cheek. Daniel grabbed her wrist and stared at her. Then he let her go and walked toward his buggy as a gentle sprinkle started to fall. By the time he reached his buggy, it was pouring.

"Daniel!"

He held a hand to his forehead to block the pounding pellets. Edna was still standing on the porch.

"Can you please stay a bit longer?" she yelled. "There are things we need to talk about."

Daniel couldn't think of one more thing he needed to say to Edna. Without answering her, he got in his buggy to make the trek toward home, his mind drifting to the possibility that the roads could start to flood. They'd already gotten a lot of rain today.

~

Annie navigated her buggy around the water pooling on the road as she made her way to Pequea Creek. It was late afternoon and the weather was horrible, but she hadn't been able to reach Jacob to reschedule. She'd even tried calling Hannah's phone, but it went straight to voice mail. She assumed cell phone usage was getting back to normal, for emergencies only. Annie's father had reminded her and Daniel that it was time to put the phones away. But the note Jacob had left her on the mailbox asking her to meet him at six at the creek had piqued her interest enough to go, despite her parents trying to talk her out of making the trip. Jacob had signed the note, *I love you with all my heart and soul.*

Thankfully, it had stopped raining by the time Annie pulled up to their picnic spot near the water's edge. Jacob's buggy was hitched to the same tree they always used, and Annie pulled up beside him. She could see Jacob sitting on a rock, his back to her. He didn't turn around as she sloshed through the mud to get to him. When she reached him, she said his name, tempted to start the conversation by fussing at him for dragging her out in this weather. But when Jacob turned around, Annie brought a hand to her chest.

"Annie . . ." Tears streamed down his face, and his entire body trembled as he stood up. "Annie . . . ," he said again, sobbing. Instinctively, she pulled him into a hug and stroked his hair like she would a child.

"I'm here, Jacob."

"Annie."

She'd never seen Jacob cry like this. She'd seen him come close, and she'd heard him get emotional on the phone, but never anything like this. As she kept her arms around him, he cried as if he'd been holding in his feelings for years. It wasn't long before Annie was crying with him.

Charlotte went to the Amish diner on Lincoln Highway at six o'clock, like Annie asked her to. It was a cute place with mostly teenage Amish girls working, and the aroma of homemade bread and cinnamon rolls hung in the air. Charlotte pulled her sweater tighter, ordered coffee, and listened to the rain pounding on the roof. It had been an awful ride in Big Red, and Charlotte was sure Annie was having a hard time in this weather. But when she'd tried to call and reschedule, there was no answer.

"Charlotte . . ."

She looked up to see Daniel standing by her table. "Hey." Sitting taller, she realized she was smiling, something she always seemed to be doing when she saw Daniel. "Sit." She pointed to the chair across from her. "Are you meeting someone or just stopping in for a quick bite to eat?"

"Both, I guess. Annie asked me to meet her here." Daniel pulled out a chair and sat down. He was soaking wet and shivering.

Charlotte tapped a finger to her chin. "She asked me to meet her here too. What do you think she wants to talk to both of us about?"

Daniel leaned his forehead against his hands and sighed. "I have no idea." Shaking his head, he said, "I hope there aren't more problems with her and Jacob."

"Me too."

Daniel ordered coffee and told the waitress they'd wait on Annie before they ordered anything. "I talked to Edna," he said. "She said she doesn't have a key to Ethan's house, and she also said she had no reason to go in it."

"Hmm . . ." Charlotte resisted the urge to make an ugly comment about Edna. "Was it awkward for you? I mean, seeing her. She wasn't at church service Sunday, but I'm assuming you see her there sometimes, or just around town, right?"

Daniel nodded. "*Ya*. As little as possible though."

"Well, thank you for checking with her." Sighing, she added, "I sure hope that house sells soon. Then I won't have to worry about anyone going in and out, and I can find a place to live. As much as I love being with Hannah and her family, I know it's not a permanent arrangement. I need my own place."

"Will you buy property or rent a house? I think there are apartments nearby as well." Daniel took off his hat and set it on the chair beside him, and Charlotte fought not to grin at his flattened dark hat hair, his cropped bangs wet and parted to the side, unintentionally for sure. She envisioned him for a few seconds as not Amish, dressed in a crisp white shirt, dark sports jacket, and slacks, his hair a bit longer. Although by Amish standards, he really needed a trim. *You are a good-looking man, Daniel Byler. Under different circumstances . . .*

"I'm not sure yet what I'll do." She gazed across the table at him. "You know what?"

He raised an eyebrow.

"I trust you more than anyone I know, except maybe Hannah and her family. Why is that?" She paused, her eyes still locked with his. "I don't trust easily."

"I don't know. But we've talked about this. I don't trust easily either, but I trust you too."

"Hmm . . . ," Charlotte said softly. "Maybe you shouldn't."

They gazed at each other across the table for a while. "Why not?" he finally asked.

Because I'm not sure if I can be trusted not to fall for a man like you. "I don't even trust me sometimes." She'd been thinking about finding a counselor here once she could afford it. She'd been making such good progress with Dr. Levin prior to the breakup with Ryan and before the recollections of the woman and girl came out of nowhere. Maybe it was time to slay her demons for good.

"You get what you see." Daniel took a sip of his coffee.

"Huh?"

"That's what you said when you said Mary Troyer was gone, only Charlotte now—what you see is what you get."

Charlotte smiled. "Oh yeah. I did say that." She pulled her eyes from Daniel's and scanned the restaurant. "Where is Annie?"

Daniel looked around also, his eyes landing back on Charlotte as he shrugged. "I don't know."

Charlotte smiled. "Did she tell you I was going to be here?"

"*Nee.*"

"She didn't mention that you might be here either. And she's not here. I do believe we've been set up."

Daniel grinned. "You think so?"

"Maybe. I sense that Annie is hoping we become more than friends."

Daniel stared at her long and hard. "Would that be such a bad thing?"

Charlotte's heart pounded against her chest. Annie's words rang in her head. *Never say never.* "It would be a disaster on so many levels."

"Ouch." Daniel's face turned as red as the truck Charlotte had arrived in. "I guess I overstepped."

"Daniel . . ." She put her palms flat on the table as she leaned forward. "Even if—" Charlotte had feelings for Daniel, but she'd worked hard to keep them in line with the way things had to be. She cleared her throat. "Never mind. The bottom line is, I'm not Amish."

After the color in Daniel's face returned to normal, he said, "You're right. It would be a disaster on so many levels."

Charlotte felt like she'd been punched in the gut. Why should it be okay for her to say it and not Daniel? Or maybe it was the way he said it. "But we'll still be friends, right?"

"Maybe."

Charlotte let out a tiny grunt. "*Maybe?*"

Daniel grinned. "You get what you see."

Fifteen

The next morning, Jacob sat beside Annie at the bus station, holding hands with her and feeling blessed. They'd found a late-night coffee shop and talked until midnight. Despite not getting much sleep, Jacob felt more rested and relaxed than he had in a long time. They'd taken a taxi to the bus station this morning. He eyed the two suitcases in front of them and wished he'd eaten breakfast. His stomach growled at him for forgetting.

Annie squeezed his hand. "Are you okay?"

Jacob nodded. Things were far from perfect, but he and Annie were united, committed to traveling wherever the Lord's path took them. The future seemed clouded by a dense fog, but light would eventually shine through and clear the way. He and Annie had prayed about the choices they were making, and they'd asked God to give them strength on their journey.

"Guess I should go." Jacob picked up both suitcases. Even though public affection was frowned upon, the feel of Annie's arm looped through his comforted his soul. It had been hard to say good-bye to his parents and Hannah this morning. He promised to write and call as often as he could. Charlotte had insisted he keep the phone she'd given him, but he planned to pay her back as soon as he got on his feet.

They stepped out onto the sidewalk where buses were loading, and Jacob turned to Annie. "The bus for Pittsburgh leaves soon." He set down the suitcases and rubbed his tired, swollen eyes. His eyelids were suddenly as heavy as his heart, but today was not a day for sissy-boy crying. He'd done enough of that the day before. He turned to Annie, closed his eyes, and kissed her with all the love in his heart.

"Pittsburgh isn't all that far," she said softly as she cupped his face.

Jacob felt eyes on them. The eyes of gaping tourists getting their first glimpses of the Amish people as they stepped off buses unloading nearby. And the locals were probably wondering about such brazenness from a young Amish couple. Jacob didn't care.

"I love you with all my heart." Jacob kissed her again.

"I'll wait for you."

Jacob didn't want to leave the comfort of her arms, but he needed to get his head right before he'd be good for anyone. His mind was filled with the desire to learn, but it wasn't just book-smarts he was seeking. He wanted to know about the world and the people in it firsthand. He felt the Lord leading him to something, and he was committed to following through.

"I will write and call as much as I can." He cupped her face in his hands and kissed her again.

Annie gazed up at him. "You frustrate me more than anyone I've ever known. But I've never loved anyone the way I love you. I want you. And I want you happy. Because when Jacob King has his head on straight, he is the most wonderful man in the world."

"I love you," he said again before one last kiss.

"And I love you."

Jacob picked up his two suitcases and forced his feet to walk toward the bus loading passengers for Pittsburgh.

Daniel shut his bedroom door and called Charlotte.

"How's everything at the King household?" he asked after she answered.

"Well, I guess okay. I heard Lena crying in her bedroom earlier. I know this is so hard on them, Jacob leaving. How's Annie?"

"Better than I thought she would be. She and Jacob have talked a lot, and they seem to have reached some sort of peace about everything." He lowered the flame on his lantern and got under the covers. "I'll check on your house tomorrow on the way to work. Are you sure you don't want me to change the locks?"

Charlotte sighed. "No, not yet. No one has damaged the property or anything. Let's just wait. That's the original hardware, those knobs. I don't want to replace them unless I absolutely have to." She was quiet for a few moments. "I hope it's not kids, runaways or something."

Daniel knew Charlotte's childhood hadn't been rosy, but she'd never shared details with him. Daniel was glad they were having a normal, easy conversation. He'd wondered if they'd be able to after their awkward chat at the diner. He cleared his throat.

"By the way, Annie did set us up. She has it in her mind that we should be more than friends." He forced himself to chuckle, an attempt to keep things light, even though his heart was beating faster. Charlotte had to know he was reaching out to her, trying to find out if she wanted to spend time with him in person. It was dangerous and stupid, but Daniel couldn't seem to stop the comment from rolling off his tongue. "I told her we already had that talk and why it would be, um—a disaster on so many levels, I think you said."

Charlotte lay on top of her covers with a hand behind her head and her ankles crossed. As she wiggled one foot back and forth, she tried to sort out the whirlwind of thoughts going through her mind. *Yes, it would be a disaster.* More upset for Daniel's family if things between her and Daniel edged into more than a friendship. But he was clearly trying to feel her out about it, or he wouldn't have brought it up.

"Maybe *disaster* was too strong a word." She squeezed her eyes closed and flinched, knowing she shouldn't encourage him. "It's not only because I'm not Amish." *Although that's certainly a large part of the mix.* She sighed. "I was seeing a counselor in Houston. Ryan paid for it." *Embarrassing.* "I guess he thought I had enough problems to warrant the sessions. But over the course of my therapy, it became clear to me that I'm carrying a lot of baggage from my childhood. I thought that if everything was good between me and Ryan, I could block out all that other stuff. But I think a good therapist has a way of dragging things to the surface. I feel like I need to fix myself before I'll be good for anyone." Her eyes widened. "Wow. I'm not sure I even realized that until right now." And it was the truth, another good reason why she and Daniel shouldn't take things to the next level. She heard laughter from outside. "I hear Hannah and Isaac outside, and I'm glad to hear Hannah laughing. She was pretty upset about Jacob earlier."

Daniel was quiet.

"You still there?"

"*Ya.* I'm here."

"Uh-oh. Did I say too much? Maybe I shouldn't have

mentioned the counseling. I promise I'm not crazy or anything. Just broken, I guess." She realized that Daniel's opinion of her mattered more than she'd known. In the darkness, she could only make out the shadows in her room, much like the thoughts in her head. Nothing was easy to see. She turned up the flame on the lantern by her bed and sat up. Crossing her legs beneath her, she waited.

"*Nee*, you didn't say too much."

And?

"And I don't think you're crazy. I think you're complicated, but in a *gut* way."

She smiled. "You get what you see, remember? I'm not sure that makes me complicated. I think you're going to need to elaborate on that."

"Hmm . . . okay. Here is what I see. You refer to yourself as broken. But I see you as seasoned. You think you have trust issues. But I see your heart on your sleeve. I see the way you help others, even if it means sacrifices for yourself. Those are all good things."

Charlotte brought a hand to her chest and waited.

"What makes you complicated is that you don't think you deserve happiness, and I can't think of anyone more deserving. I feel like God has His hand on you and is touching you in ways you don't completely understand."

"I didn't grow up as a faithful child of God. Last time I was here, in Lancaster County, I found God and invited Him into my life." Pausing, she took a deep breath. "He has bulldozed His way into my life and heart, and sometimes I feel overwhelmed. And yes, sometimes I do feel undeserving of His love and acceptance."

"It's unconditional, Charlotte—God's love. None of us are deserving, but God's love is like a deep well that never dries up. There are no droughts where the Lord is concerned. Ask, and it shall be given you; seek, and ye shall find; knock, and it shall be opened unto you."

"I have been asking God to show me the way, but sometimes I feel like I'm in a tunnel, wondering if there's any light at the end." She reached for a tissue and dabbed at her eyes. "I'm not sure He is hearing me. When does peace come?"

"On God's time frame."

Daniel offered to pray with Charlotte, and as she bowed her head, she thanked God . . . for Daniel.

Annie put a hand over her mouth to stifle a gasp. "You're where? Is it a safe place?" she whispered from her dark bedroom.

"Listen to how it happened," Jacob said. "I was standing on the sidewalk, not far from the bus station. There was a motel with a flashing light that said twenty-two dollars for the night. I felt like the luckiest guy ever to find a room for that price. I was just about to take advantage of my good luck when a man came up to me and said he didn't think that motel was somewhere I should stay. He was dressed all in black and had stepped out of a black car by the curb, a real long car with tinted windows."

"Were you scared?"

"I was hungry."

Annie rolled her eyes but grinned. "What happened?"

"I told him I was trying to be careful with my money, and I asked him what was wrong with this place. He was old, like *mei daed*'s age. He was dressed real nice in *Englisch* clothes, but he had some gray hair and wrinkles. I didn't wear suspenders or my straw hat, but maybe my clothes and haircut gave me away. He asked if I was Amish. I said I was. Then he handed me a fancy business card, all black with gold writing. He told me to go three blocks up the road, to check into that hotel, and to tell them the big rabbit sent me."

"The big rabbit?"

"*Ya*, weird, huh? I thought about waiting until he left and just going on into the cheap motel, but he waited, even offered me a ride."

"Please tell me you didn't take a ride from a strange *Englisch* man in a car with windows you can't see through." Annie squeezed her eyes closed and said more prayers that the Lord would keep Jacob safe.

"Well, I wasn't going to, but my suitcases were heavy and he seemed okay."

Annie shook her head and waited.

"Anyway, he dropped me at the hotel, a really, really big hotel, Annie. And he told me again to tell them the big rabbit sent me. I thanked him and got out. So I walked into this place called the Omni William Penn Hotel. Annie, I ain't ever seen anything like this place in my life, even on television. I think famous or royal people must stay here."

Annie was quiet.

"I walked up to a long counter with several people standing behind it. I went to where a woman stood behind the counter, and I felt so dumb, but I said the big rabbit sent me. She narrowed her eyebrows at me, frowned, and said, 'Excuse me?' Then I got scared, figuring the man had done me dirty or something. I didn't know what to do. But then another man who was near her walked to her side and asked me what I'd said. Still feeling dumb, I said it again."

Annie took in a deep breath as she listened.

"Next thing I know, a man in a fancy black suit is picking up my suitcases and taking me to an elevator. We went to the fourth floor, and he opened my door and carried in my suitcases." Jacob laughed out loud. "He told me to order anything I wanted from room service, and when I asked how much that would cost, he said it was free." Jacob chuckled again. "And you should see this room . . ."

Annie listened as Jacob described his fancy hotel room. She was glad he wasn't sad or sounding desperate and afraid. And she'd agreed to give him some time to sort out his thoughts to see where things stood with them.

But this attraction to such fanciness was not their way, not at all.

He was going on about all the things in the room. The big television, small refrigerator, bar, desk, computer for his use, phone—the list went on and on. "Why would this man do this for you? He's a stranger. I don't understand."

"Maybe he's an angel," Jacob said, chattering more about the room. "When the man in the suit left, he said I could stay here as long as I want. For *free*."

"I don't understand," she said again.

"This is my path, Annie. God led this kind man to me to make sure I had food and shelter. It's like a miracle. I was worried about how long my money would last, but now I have a free place to stay while I look for a job. Isn't that great?"

Annie thought about the awful shape Jacob had been in before he left. Now he was the happiest man in the world. His moods shifted from one extreme to another. And more often than the moods of anyone she'd ever known. He'd always been like that, but the past couple of months, his moods seemed more extreme.

"I'm a blessed man," Jacob said softly.

Annie wasn't so sure. In the pit of her stomach was a rumbling of nerves that told her something just wasn't right.

Following a restless night, Annie met her mother in the kitchen the next morning. "*Mamm*, let me clean the kitchen while you rest." She'd noticed the bags under her mother's eyes and how much she'd slowed down since she found out she was pregnant. The doctor said *Mamm* was four months along and that everything was going well.

"*Nee, nee.* It will go faster with two of us." Her mother filled the sink with soapy water while Annie cleared the table. "Did you talk to Jacob yesterday? Did he arrive in Pittsburgh all right? I'm glad he decided not to go very far." *Mamm* shook her head. "I don't understand that lad."

Me either. "*Ya*, he got there in the evening, and an *Englisch* stranger helped him get a hotel room, a really fancy room."

"I don't agree with Jacob's choices." *Mamm* turned the water off and took a stack of plates from Annie, submerging them in the bubbles. "Hopefully he will get all this silliness out of his head and come back here. But"—she turned to Annie—"there are other fish in the sea, as the *Englisch* folks say."

"I don't want another fish." Annie pulled a dish towel from the drawer. "I want Jacob to get back to normal. He's been so depressed." *Until last night.*

"I've wondered about Jacob over the years. Even when he was a little boy, he always had a book in his hand, and he talked about things that seemed well beyond his years.

I know his *mudder* always worried that he might leave here someday."

"I think it's just something he needs to get out of his system. I hope so, anyway." Annie pictured Jacob in his fancy hotel room, probably watching television, enjoying the electricity, and eating free food. "Where did Daniel go? He said he didn't have any work for today, but I saw him leave in his buggy after breakfast."

"He went to check on Charlotte's little house. He said someone has been going in and out."

"Oh no. Breaking in? Is anything damaged?"

Annie dried a plate and set it on the counter, taking another dish from her mother.

"Daniel said there's no vandalism. He thinks someone is staying there at night, though."

Annie frowned. "Who would do that?"

Her mother shrugged. "I don't know. He doesn't know either." She paused, holding a spatula in her hand. "He talks to Charlotte a lot. I can't decide how I feel about that."

"I think it's wonderful." Annie smiled. "I wish they'd start dating."

Mamm huffed. "What? She's not Amish. How can you say that? You do remember she was only pretending to be Amish while she was here last year. That girl told a lot of lies. I know she was very *gut* to Lena during her chemo treatments, and she was also *gut* to you and Jacob, but I'm not sure I'd choose her for Daniel. I wish her the best." *Mamm* glanced at Annie. "But you should get that notion out of your head."

Annie carried a stack of plates to the other end of the counter and opened the cabinet. "Charlotte is wonderful, *Mamm*. I'd love to have her as my sister-in-law. She understands our ways, respects them, and she's really smart. And pretty."

"Please don't encourage your *bruder* in that direction. I need at least one of *mei kinner* to choose wisely." *Mamm* grinned.

"Jacob will come around. I know he will." And that's what Annie planned to keep telling herself.

Sixteen

Daniel was glad to find the door locked at Charlotte's house. He pulled the key from his pocket and opened it. He scanned the living room and then walked to the kitchen. Everything was in place. But when he went into the bedroom, he saw a can of Dr Pepper, some gum wrappers, and a couple of needles on the floor. Definitely not insulin needles.

Their people avoided calling the law unless absolutely necessary, but he suspected that whoever was coming in and out might be an unsavory character. Maybe the intruder was a runaway whose frantic parents were somewhere worrying. Whoever it was, they were entering private property without permission.

He rechecked the windows. All locked. He looked out back but saw no trash or anything out of the ordinary. After walking back into the house, he went to the bedroom again and took another look around. He decided to leave everything where it was on the floor. Maybe instead of calling the police, he should come back at night. He wasn't sure how he'd be able to sneak up to the place without whoever was inside seeing him. He hesitated, not wanting the real estate company to show the house with needles on the floor. He decided to carefully get rid of the needles but leave the gum wrappers and soda can. Maybe whoever was coming in and out wouldn't notice what was or wasn't left behind.

After disposing of the needles, he locked the door, then walked across the yard toward his buggy. He noticed the flower beds void of any spring growth, weeds sprouting instead. He should ask Annie to come plant some flowers here to spruce things up a bit. Annie cared for Charlotte, and it might help to sell the house. But he tossed the thought, not really wanting Annie coming here if someone was sneaking in at night. It was best that Annie not take any chances.

Jacob was sure he'd just had the best sleep of his life, despite his circumstances. Maybe it was the squishy mattress, satin sheets, and Jacuzzi. He smiled as he dove into a huge breakfast of pancakes, scrambled eggs, bacon, sausage, hash browns, and biscuits.

He needed to start looking for a job, but surely no

one could fault him for taking a day to settle in. Clicking on the television with the remote control, he thought about Annie. She would likely say this room was way too fancy, that the food wasn't nearly as good as at home, and that this was all luxury that they didn't need. But he was pretty sure that Annie would watch the TV.

He jumped when there was a knock at the door and quickly set the tray of food aside. He slipped into his black slacks and threw on his shirt, buttoning it on the way to the door as his bare feet hurried across the plush beige carpet. The same man from the night before was on the other side of the threshold, the man responsible for all of Daniel's good fortune. "Hello, Big Rabbit," he said. "*Danki* for all you've done for me." He stepped aside so the man could come in. "Excuse my untidiness," he added, nodding to the tray of food on the bed, socks and shoes on the floor, and newspaper spread out at the foot of the bed.

The man smiled. "No worries." Then he chuckled. "And Big Rabbit is not my name, merely a code for my guests to use when they check in." He extended his hand to Daniel. "My name is Liam Stone."

Jacob shook the man's hand. "I'm Jacob King."

"Did you sleep well, Jacob? Is there anything you need?" The man was shorter than Jacob, and he wasn't dressed in black today. Instead, he wore gray slacks and a pink short-sleeved shirt with fancy gray loafers. In the light of day, he was able to see him better, and his short dark hair was sprinkled with more gray than Jacob had noticed the night before. More wrinkles too. But he had a friendly face when he smiled and bright white teeth.

"I slept real *gut*," Jacob said, wondering if he'd have enough money to buy clothes like Liam was wearing. He needed to work harder to sound like an *Englisch* person too.

"Are you running away from home, Jacob King?" The man smiled a little as he raised one eyebrow.

"*Nee, nee.* No, sir. I'm not running away. My family knows that I'm in Pittsburgh. This is my time as a teenager to try out the *Englisch* world, I guess you could say."

"And might I ask how old you are?"

"I'll be eighteen in three months."

The man walked to the end of the bed and picked up a section of the newspaper. "You are searching for work?" The man held up the classifieds.

"*Ya.* I mean yes. Yes, I'm looking for a job."

"And what is an almost-eighteen-year-old Amish lad qualified to do?"

Jacob detected a tiny bit of sarcasm, but this man had been mighty good to him so far. "Not much of anything, I'm afraid. I've spent my life farming. I'm pretty good at building furniture. And I know how to operate a cash register. I'm real *gut* at math. And I read a lot."

"The Amish only go to school through the eighth grade, correct?"

Jacob avoided the man's eyes as he felt his face get

warm. "*Ya* . . . I mean yes. But I kept up with my studies after that. I've read hundreds of books, and I know how to do calculus."

"Well, well," the man said, smiling again. "Impressive." He rubbed his clean-shaven chin. "Perhaps we can talk job opportunities."

Thank You, God, for these abundant blessings. "That would be great."

Friday night, Daniel held his cell phone in his hand with Charlotte's number in view. He was trying to decide whether or not to call her—knowing it would only stir up trouble—when someone knocked on his bedroom door.

"It's me. Can I come in?" Annie said before she opened the door a little bit, then waited.

"Looks like you're coming in anyway," Daniel said, putting the phone on the nightstand.

Annie walked in dressed in her nightgown and robe. "Sorry. I know it's late, but I figured you'd be up." She grinned. "Talking to Charlotte on the phone."

"What are you getting at, Annie?" Daniel crossed his ankles. Annie sat down in the chair against the far wall. Daniel yawned, knowing if he was going to call Charlotte, it would have to be soon.

Annie batted her eyelashes, shrugging. "I'm not getting at anything. I think it's great that the two of you are friends." She pushed her long hair over her shoulders. "Do you think you'll become more than friends?"

"I don't think this is a conversation you and I should be having."

"Why not? I'm your sister. I'm grown up. I'm seventeen."

Daniel twisted his mouth into a half smile. "Whatever you say. How's Jacob?" Best to get this conversation going in another direction. Daniel figured that's why Annie was still up this late anyway.

Annie sat taller and lifted her chin. "Jacob is in a fancy hotel living the lavish lifestyle of the *Englisch*, filled with waste and extravagance, and I don't know how I feel about that."

"Where'd you learn a word like *extravagance*?" Daniel held up a hand. "Never mind. Jacob, I'm sure. And I doubt Jacob has enough money to be spending it on a fancy hotel. He'll be back before you know it, when he runs out of money."

Annie shook her head. "*Nee*, he is staying in this hotel for free. And he's eating for free too." She filled him in on the recent events. "Jacob thinks the man is an angel or something. As of earlier today, the man had even offered Jacob a job. He didn't share details with me, but . . ." She sighed. "Jacob is embracing that lifestyle."

"That's what he did in Houston, too, but it didn't take him long to tire of it, and he'll tire of it again." Daniel yawned. "Maybe he'll grow up now."

"You used to love Jacob." Annie's bottom lip turned under, and Daniel reminded himself of how much Annie had been through lately.

"I still love Jacob. But he needs to grow up, and until he does, I'm not sure he's the best man for you, Annie. That's all I'm saying."

"I was really worried about him, Daniel. When we met and talked at the coffee shop the night before last, he was a mess. He'd been crying most of the day. And he broke down with me at the creek before that. It scared me. It made me think about . . ." She lowered her head, then lifted her eyes to his. "It made me think about Ethan."

"Do you think Jacob is suicidal?" Daniel wished he didn't even have to ask the question, but after Ethan's death, they all became concerned when someone was overly depressed.

"I never would have, until I saw how upset he was that night. Jacob gets really, really happy, but then he can get really, really sad. His moods go back and forth."

"I know you're worried about him," Daniel said softly. "Try to get some sleep. God is watching over him."

"That's what Jacob keeps saying, but I have a weird feeling. Something just isn't right."

Annie hugged him good night and kissed him on the cheek before she headed to her bedroom. Daniel lay in bed for a few minutes before he called Charlotte. Thankfully, he had a purpose for the call.

"How's Jacob?" she asked after she answered. "Has Annie talked to him?"

"Annie was just in my room. She's worried about him." Daniel told Charlotte about Jacob's adventures since his arrival in Pittsburgh two days ago.

"Daniel, that doesn't sound good," she said. "I agree with Annie. Something isn't right."

"Sometimes people just do nice things for other people. The man sounds very wealthy, and he saw an Amish kid getting ready to check into a run-down motel. He did a *gut* deed."

"Maybe."

"What worries me, though, is that Annie told me how depressed Jacob has been, how it made her think about Ethan."

Charlotte didn't say anything.

Daniel leaned his head back against his pillow, closed his eyes, and sighed. "Listen, I found some other things at the house. I didn't mention them before because I didn't want you to worry more than you already are."

"Like what?" Charlotte sounded like she'd come to attention.

"When I told you about the chicken box and toilet paper, I found some other things in the trash outside, the stuff that got scattered by some critter."

"What did you find?" More urgency in her voice. "Tell me."

"Some needles, not the kind diabetics use. I briefly

thought about Jacob. There was this day he looked a little drunk. I'd mentioned it to Hannah. But I don't see Jacob doing anything like that. I think a better explanation is that a homeless person is sleeping there, a young person, I think. There were a bunch of gum wrappers and soda cans—Dr Pepper. And someone likes to doodle. I found scraps of paper with stars drawn all over them. The first time, I packed it all up and took it out. But today when I checked on the place, there was more of the same stuff. And that's odd. You'd think whoever was going in and out would realize they'd been caught when the things they'd left there were gone."

Daniel waited for Charlotte to respond. "You still there?"

"Yes. I'm just thinking."

"You're worried it's a young person, a runaway or something?"

He waited, but she remained quiet.

"What are you thinking?"

"Daniel . . ." Her voice was meek and shaky. "What kind of gum?"

He felt lost. "What does it matter what kind of gum?"

"What kind of gum?" she asked a little louder, but still with a tremble in her voice.

"Uh . . ." He tried to remember. "Juicy Fruit or something to do with fruit."

"Was it Fruit Stripe?" she asked, whimpering slightly.

Daniel tried to remember. "It might have been. The

packaging had striped colors. Why? Please tell me what's wrong."

"I think I know who is going in my house, Ethan's house."

Daniel stopped breathing. "Who?"

~

Charlotte was already pulling her jeans on. "I'm going over there, to the house."

"Tonight?"

If her suspicions were on target, she wouldn't be able to sleep. "Yes."

"Well, come pick me up. I'm not letting you go over there by yourself." When she didn't respond, he said, "Charlotte, did you hear me? You can't over there by yourself."

"Okay." She was too nervous to argue with him and not thrilled about going by herself anyway. And touched that he was worried.

After she pulled her shirt over her head and found her flip-flops, she moved toward the door as quietly as she could, although not much woke up Hannah lately. Her friend had taken to wearing earplugs. Hannah said she'd worn them in the past when she had trouble sleeping, but Charlotte suspected it might be the *clickety-click* of the keyboard on Charlotte's computer at night. *Or maybe I snore?*

For now, Charlotte's challenge would be to get out of the house without Buddy barking. She still couldn't believe the way Buddy and Amos had taken to each other.

She scribbled a note about where she was going and left it on the kitchen table, even though she hoped to be back way before everyone was up. Once she'd made a clean getaway, she cranked up the old truck. *Please don't wake up, Buddy.*

By the time she pulled up to Daniel's house, she'd bitten two of her nails down to the quick, something she hadn't done since she was a kid.

He was outside when she pulled up and was in the truck within a few seconds. He put his hand on her arm. "Are you okay?"

Charlotte threw caution to the wind and leaned into his arms, sure she'd never needed a hug more than now. Maybe in the darkness he wouldn't see the circles under her eyes or notice how pale she was. He held her tightly and smoothed her hair with his hand, the way a loving mother soothes a child.

Charlotte stayed in the comfort of his arms. "I'm scared," was all she managed to choke out.

"Everything is going to be okay," he whispered. "And I'm not going to let anything happen to you. Do you hear me?" He eased her away just as a tear slipped down her cheek. Brushing it away, he kissed her on the forehead. "You're okay, *ya*?"

She definitely wasn't okay, but she nodded, took a

deep breath, and put the truck in reverse, then slammed right into the barn. "No, no, no." She glanced over her shoulder. "I'm so sorry! I'm sorry! I didn't see it. I'm sorry!" She was yelling and crying at the same time.

Daniel's mouth hung open for a few seconds, his eyes wide. Then he calmly spoke. "Charlotte, it's just a barn. It's okay." Frowning, he said, "Do you want me to drive since you're so upset?"

In spite of the circumstances, she chuckled. "You've asked me that before, and I'm pretty sure you said you don't know how to drive."

He smiled, and Charlotte wished she could stay with him in the truck forever. "How hard can it be?" he asked.

They needed the light moment. She laughed a little, swiped at her tears, and got out to check the damage. Daniel did too. The barn was fine, and another dent or scratch on the truck would have gone unnoticed. They got resituated, and Charlotte headed down the driveway. A few minutes later, she turned right, toward the place Ethan used to call home. They were almost there when Charlotte pulled to the side of the road, trembling. Two buggies passed them, unusual for this time of night, but not unheard of. All the buggies were required to have headlights to drive in the dark. "I just need a minute," she said as she reminded herself to breathe, gulping in air as if there was a shortage.

"Take all the time you need."

Charlotte could feel an onslaught of tears trying to

come on again. She wiped beneath her eyes with her fingers, then pulled back onto the road. When they got to the entrance of Ethan's driveway, Charlotte cut the engine. They got out to walk the rest of the way, hoping to go unnoticed if someone was inside.

"This is probably so stupid," she said as they followed the flashlight Daniel kept pointed at the ground.

Daniel latched onto her hand and squeezed it three times. Charlotte knew what that meant in her world. But did it mean the same thing to him? She reminded herself not to lead him on, even though she cared about him a lot. But were she and Daniel as star-crossed as Annie and Jacob when it came to matters of the heart? There was a spark between them, no doubt.

"Do you want me to go in first?" Daniel asked when they reached the front yard. "There's a light coming from inside, Charlotte. It looks like it's coming from the bedroom. Maybe you should wait out here."

Charlotte shook her head. "No. I'll go too."

They walked the rest of the way across the yard and tiptoed up the porch steps, and Charlotte reached for the doorknob. "It's locked."

Daniel took the key from his pocket and put it in the lock.

Charlotte's head spun, and she felt like everything was moving in slow motion as they stepped over the threshold and fumbled their way through the living room, inching toward the bedroom, which had gone dark.

Daniel stayed beside her, holding the flashlight, the only potential weapon they had if they needed it. And would Daniel even use it to protect them? The Amish avoided fighting at all costs. But when he stepped in front of her, shielding her from danger, she knew he'd do whatever it took to protect her.

He shined the flashlight around the bedroom as Charlotte peeked around him. Her eyes landed on a few Fruit Stripe gum wrappers, a Dr Pepper can, and . . . a syringe. No drawings or doodles. And no person.

She started to tremble. The gum wrappers and soda can—along with the star sketches Daniel had described before—could all be a coincidence. But someone had been here. Daniel continued to shine the light around the room.

"Maybe the person moved to another part of the house," Daniel whispered.

Charlotte nodded toward the closet door, where she was pretty sure she'd heard a movement. Daniel opened the door, and a flashlight clicked on and someone lurched toward him, then past him. But Daniel caught the woman's arm before she reached Charlotte, keeping a firm hold on her.

"Let me go! I have a right to be here!" The woman wiggled, her flashlight throwing shadows around the room. She kicked at Daniel, trying to free his hold.

"Janell?" Charlotte's legs turned to jelly as her heart rate sped up. She couldn't move.

The woman stopped struggling, even though Daniel still held tightly to her arm. "How do you know my name?"

It had been at least ten years since Charlotte last saw Janell, but no amount of speculating could have prepared her for this. Janell was a tiny bag of bones, pale, with dark circles under her eyes. She was dressed in blue jeans and a plain white T-shirt. Her dark hair hung almost to her shoulders, tucked behind her ears and speckled with more salt than pepper. Thinning lips gave way to sunken cheeks.

Charlotte had thought about what she'd say to Janell a hundred times, but she couldn't formulate a sentence now.

"What do you want? I said I have a right to be here." She peered at Charlotte. "Do I know you?"

Charlotte recalled all the times she'd seen Janell smacking on fruity gum and drinking Dr Pepper. Sometimes she'd doodle stars until she passed out. She glanced at the needle on the floor. If Janell had been shooting up anything back then, Charlotte couldn't remember. But she remembered Janell's other habits. *Memories. Selective, perhaps.*

"I knew the man who lived here," Janell spat at Charlotte. "It's fine for me to be in his house." She nodded toward the needle, gum wrappers, and soda can. "And that's not my stuff."

Charlotte recognized on Janell's face the pitted sores of a meth user, along with her discolored, rotting teeth and dilated eyes. She remembered the look of a methamphetamine addict from her time in foster care, long before the illegal drug became widely popular.

"Can you tell this brute of an Amish man to let go of me?" Janell tried to pull away again, but Daniel held on to her until she quit struggling.

"Janell, do you know who I am?" Charlotte prayed for strength, for the right words, and for her legs not to give out.

Janell rolled her eyes. "I haven't a clue."

Charlotte didn't try to stop the tear that rolled down her cheek. Something about not being recognized by her own mother was too much to bear. "Janell. It's me. Charlotte." *Face the demons.* Memories bubbled to the surface, recollections that were best left in the dark recesses of Charlotte's mind.

Janell smiled. She was missing a tooth about a third of the way back on the upper left. "*My* Charlotte?" she said in a whimper as her body went limp. Daniel let go of her arm, but he stayed by Janell's side as Charlotte's mother took a step toward her. "My baby girl, Charlotte?"

"I'm not a little girl anymore." *And I wasn't the last time you saw me either.* Charlotte remembered a time when she'd called Janell "Mom," but even in her thoughts, the woman was Janell, someone unworthy of the title. An abusive drunk who'd lost both of her children for a while, then later stepped out of their lives completely.

Charlotte assumed that her anger at her parents would direct her actions if she ever saw either one of them and drive her to a hysterical display of emotion. But as she stared at the woman in front of her, all she felt was pity. Charlotte wondered if she should have made attempts to find Janell sooner, like her therapist had suggested—if not for Charlotte's own good, for Janell's. She could come up with a hundred reasons why the answer to that question was no.

When Janell walked toward her with outstretched arms, Daniel moved along with her, but Charlotte took a step backward.

Janell stopped, lowered her arms to her sides, and started to cry. "You are my beautiful baby girl, Charlotte. You are my child, my flesh and blood. My daughter." She smiled through her tears.

Janell slowly moved toward Charlotte, and this time Charlotte didn't move when Janell wrapped her arms around her. But Charlotte kept her arms at her sides, trying not to gag from the smell of an unwashed body.

Janell eased away, and her smile faded until there was no expression left on her face. "Ethan is dead. He killed himself."

Charlotte glanced at Daniel, then back at Janell. "Yes, I know."

Janell picked at a spot on her cheek. "Your father is dead too. Shot in the head in a barroom brawl. At least that's what I heard."

Charlotte hugged herself tightly, hung her head, and cried. Probably not the way anyone wanted to learn of their father's death, no matter how bad a guy he was.

"I'm surprised you have any tears to spare for him," Janell said, sniffling. "After the way he treated us and all." She moved to another spot on her face and poked at it with her finger, her nails bitten to the quick.

Charlotte rubbed her thumbs against her own chewed nails. *What about the way you treated us?*

"So, how are you, Charlotte? Do you and Ethan spend a lot of time together?"

Charlotte looked at Janell. "What?"

"I think it's so good when siblings stay close."

Charlotte looked at Daniel, who was standing within an arm's reach behind Charlotte's mother, but he shrugged, a pained expression on his face. Charlotte looked back at the woman who had given birth to her and her brother. "Ethan is dead. Remember?"

Janell's eyes grew wide, and she began picking at her face until it bled. "My boy is dead?"

Charlotte nodded.

Janell covered her face with her hands and sobbed. "My Ethan is dead." She uncovered her face and gasped. "Did you kill him?"

Charlotte had known people who'd abused meth. This was starting to look like more than a drug addiction. She'd been praying constantly, but right now, Charlotte needed God to be here, in this room, with her. She needed Him to hold her up and to show her the way. "Lord, give me strength. No, Janell, I did not kill Ethan."

Janell smiled. "I am so glad to hear that. And it makes me happy to hear you talk to God. I talk with God all the time." She shook her head, frowning. "I don't think He hears me."

Charlotte swiped at her eyes, sniffled, and looked at the floor where Daniel had the flashlight pointed, wondering if the darkness in her heart would be replaced by light now that she was facing her demons.

"He hears you, Janell." Charlotte held out her hand. Slowly Janell took it, her hands rough like a ninety-year-old woman's might be. "This isn't a good place for you to stay. Let's go get you cleaned up, and we'll find somewhere better."

Janell shuffled barefoot alongside Charlotte, holding her hand. Daniel got in step behind them.

"Is Ethan coming?" Janell asked as they crossed through the living room.

"No, Mom."

Seventeen

It was three in the morning when Charlotte dropped Daniel off at home. They'd said very little to each other after they'd left Janell at the rehabilitation facility. Charlotte was exhausted, and she knew Daniel must be, too, even though he never complained. He had stayed by Charlotte's side through every step of the process: the paperwork, evaluations, and questions. He had also endured the intolerable smell in the truck as they drove her from one hospital to the next until they found a place that would take her with no insurance.

Eventually she was accepted at a state-run agency for people who were mentally ill, but it would also be a place to wean her body off the drugs she'd taken for so long. But it was only a month-long program. Charlotte would try to find a more permanent solution after she had some time to think. But Janell's temporary home wasn't a lock-in facility. Janell could walk out anytime she wanted, even though she'd promised Charlotte she would stay.

"I don't know how I'll ever thank you," Charlotte said to Daniel as she pulled into his driveway.

"No thanks required." He smiled, but tired gray eyes looked back at her, and Charlotte knew his mind was filled with questions. They'd held hands, and Charlotte had clung to him, even completely broken down in his arms once they'd left Janell.

Charlotte hugged him bye and kissed him on the cheek, lingering in his arms for longer than she probably should have. After trying to assure him that she would be okay, they parted ways. She managed to get back in the house without waking up Buddy and made her way upstairs, falling on the bed in her clothes. She buried her face in her pillow and wept as quietly as she could, hoping not to wake up Hannah.

After a few hours of sleep and a bath, she went downstairs and tearfully told Lena, Amos, and Hannah about her mother.

"So my mother is at a psychiatric hospital for a month until I can figure out what to do with her. And apparently, my father is dead." She glanced at each of them. Hannah was dabbing at her eyes. Amos was staring at the floor. Lena walked from where she'd been standing, sat down on the other side of Charlotte, and pulled her into her arms.

"Sweet *maedel*, everything is going to be all right. We are here for you." She eased away from Charlotte, brushed back the hair from across her face, and kissed her on the cheek.

Charlotte nodded, crying harder. "I don't know what I'd do without any of you." She glanced at Amos, but he was still looking down. Charlotte wondered if Amos would ever open his heart to her again.

She took a deep breath. "The lady at the hospital said they'd assign us a social worker. Since Janell isn't a resident of Pennsylvania, I don't know what type of state-funded options might be available to us." Charlotte recognized that she was using the word *us*, which seemed strange in light of the situation. "I guess I'll just take things one day at a time." She shrugged. "Who knows if Janell will even stay in rehab."

"Where's she been living when she wasn't staying in Ethan's house?" Hannah asked.

"I can't get many straight answers, but it sounds like she bounced from one person's place to another, wherever she could find to lay her head. She'd found out only recently that Ethan died. I don't know how or from whom, but she said she felt called by God to come here. I don't believe that. I think she probably came to see if she had any rights to anything he owned. She said she hitchhiked. I don't know if I believe that either. She had two hundred dollars in her purse, which is odd. But it takes money to buy drugs." Charlotte had her theories about how Janell had been surviving, but she'd said enough. "There were two original keys to the house. One was under the mat, and Janell found it and kept it, admitting she sometimes forgot to lock the door."

"Isaac used to leave a key under the mat so his workers could come in on days he wasn't there. Maybe he forgot and left a copy there," Hannah said. "I remember that because it was hard having the key made. It's an old-timey key or something."

"Yeah. That's the reason the real estate company couldn't put a lockbox on the door."

"I'm so glad you decided to move here." Hannah crossed her hands over her chest, smiling. "We can help you take care of your mother, Charlotte."

Charlotte's eyes darted to Amos again. He was staring past Charlotte, as if deep in thought. She turned to Lena. "I don't know when or why, but somewhere in this mess, I've decided I want to take Ethan's house off the market. I don't know what the future holds. If my mom is willing, she needs long-term rehab. But I need to stand on my own, too, absorb Jesus' strength, and . . . something about selling Ethan's house doesn't feel right anymore." She'd gotten a couple of checks, and she was more productive here. After the dust settled, and if she ever felt a sense of normalcy again, she'd hit social media hard to try to round up more editing jobs. "When I can afford it, I'll have electricity installed."

Lena smiled. "I think you've been doing very well

here without electricity, and we surely have lanterns and other necessities to get you started. But this is not a time for making big decisions," Lena said. "The situation with your mother requires your immediate attention. Everything else will work out, all in God's perfect time."

Charlotte thought about how the events of her life were unfolding. What would have happened if things had gone any other way? When Ryan broke up with her, she'd begged God for another chance with him, even though it was surely best that they didn't reconcile. Charlotte had considered herself unworthy of love, assumed God wasn't hearing her prayers. She was learning to trust Him more as her life took twists and turns that she didn't always understand. She recalled all the prayers she'd said for Daniel, grateful he'd been praying for her too.

"You can stay here as long as you'd like," Lena said with all the love and comfort of a mother. Charlotte glanced at Amos, waiting for a reaction from him, but his head was down.

"You've all been through so much with Jacob. I don't want to be a burden or cause more drama in your lives. And besides, I think it will be good for me to be on my own."

Lena's expression fell. "We are sad about Jacob, and we say extra prayers that he will find his way onto God's intended path for him, no matter what that might be. But you bring joy into our lives."

Charlotte smiled. "I'll still be close by." She still couldn't believe that her mother was back in her life.

"As you wish," Lena said. "Hannah and I must go make some deliveries to a few of the shut-ins in our area. We started baking early this morning and have everything packed in the kitchen. Do you want to come with us, or would you prefer to rest?"

"Actually, I think I'll lag behind if that's okay."

Charlotte helped Hannah and Lena load their buggy and told them again that she'd be fine. And it was the truth. She felt like load-bearing walls had been crumbling around her for years, crushing her a little bit at a time. But when the ceiling finally came down, threatening to flatten and destroy her for good, she was suddenly infused with a superpower that had given her the strength of Job. And there was only one superpower, God the Father. *Thank You, Lord.*

When she went back into the house, Amos and Buddy had disappeared into the bedroom. Charlotte found her purse and left to go see Daniel, knowing he didn't have to work on Saturdays. But running an Amish farm often required lots of chores even on weekends. She'd tried to call, but no one answered. Again, she assumed the cell phone usage was returning to normal for her Plain friends.

Daniel was coming out of the barn, wiping his hands on a rag, when she pulled up. He hurried toward her, and as Charlotte flung the truck door open, her legs carried her straight into his arms. Their embrace lasted awhile before Charlotte eased away. "Sorry. I—I just wanted to see you. I just . . ." She blinked a few times.

Daniel touched her cheek tenderly, his eyes meeting hers. "I'm glad you came. And we don't have to figure everything out right this minute." He eased his hand away and smiled.

She didn't have any regrets about getting to know him. Her growing feelings for him scared her, but over the course of her young life, she'd been scared plenty of times, and she was beginning to believe she was braver than she ever imagined. "That's what Lena said, that I don't have to figure everything out right now. But I have decided to take Ethan's house off the market, then clean it top to bottom before I start moving my things in."

"Are you sure you're ready to do that?"

Charlotte nodded. "Yeah. I am."

Daniel's serious expression seemed a prelude to something he was about to say, but he just stared at her. "Are you okay? You must be really tired still."

He inched toward her and leaned down slightly, and Charlotte wondered if he was going to kiss her. She'd let him, even though it would further complicate things. In Amish country, a kiss could take things from zero to everything, and she was too broken to drag Daniel into her mess any more than he already was. She needed to tell him that one of the main reasons she moved to Lancaster County was because she'd been evicted, but shame wrapped around her and she stayed quiet.

~

Daniel stared into Charlotte's eyes, unsure of the exact moment he'd started to care so much for her. His feelings had snuck up on him, and he knew he was setting himself up for heartache by getting involved with an *Englisch* woman. Charlotte had a world of issues, things she needed to work through. And now this situation with her mother. But he leaned forward until his lips met hers, and all those thoughts flew out of his mind. His heart led the way, and as she kissed him back, he lost himself completely in her.

"I've wanted to do that for a long time," he said softly as he cupped her cheek.

She stared up into his eyes. "It seems an understatement to tell you what a wonderful friend you've been to me." She bit her bottom lip. "But Daniel, I'm a bit of a mess."

He smiled. "*Ya*, I know."

She rolled her eyes, grinning. "You could have argued with me."

Daniel would recall the sensation of her lips against his for a long time, but Charlotte needed time to get used to all the changes in her life too. "You have many things to think about and take care of, I know this."

She nodded, still gazing up at him. "I think you know how much I care about you." She looked away, then back at him. "I'm not Amish."

I've laid awake nights reminding myself of this. "Are you sure?"

She squinted at him. "What?"

"*Ach*, well . . . awhile back, you dressed Amish during your time here." He smiled, letting her know that he was way past that situation and had more than forgiven her. "You have a strong faith," he added. "And now you are moving into a *haus* with no electricity or modern conveniences. That sounds pretty Amish to me."

She laughed. "I guess it does."

Daniel kissed her forehead. "Rest, Charlotte. Get things settled with your *mudder* and get moved into your new home. We will all help you with that." He smiled, touching her lightly on the cheek. "I'm not going anywhere."

Charlotte smiled. "Me either." She opened the truck door, but before she got in, she said, "Give Annie my love. I know this is a tough time for her."

Daniel nodded. In truth, his sister was making them all a little crazy, pacing the house and waiting for Jacob to call her.

After devotions with her parents, Annie lingered downstairs, hoping Daniel would be home soon. He'd been gone all afternoon, and now it was evening. Someone had ordered a shed to be delivered and set up, and they'd paid a hefty price for a one-day turnaround—on a Sunday.

She paced the living room, looking out the window into the darkness, then walked into the kitchen, then back to the living room, praying he'd get home soon. It was easier to talk to her brother than her parents.

Her father shook his head, frowning. "I know you are waiting for that boy to call you from his chosen life in the *Englisch* world, but all of this must stop," he said without looking up from a book he'd just opened. "All these phone calls . . ." He grumbled something under his breath. Annie sat down on the couch so she wouldn't upset her father more.

Her mother reached into her knitting basket and went to work on a pair of pink booties she was making.

"What if the baby is a boy?" Annie tucked her legs underneath her on the couch.

"It's a girl," her mother said, not lifting her eyes from her project.

Annie brought a hand to her chest and gasped slightly. "*Mamm*, did you have the test like the *Englisch* do, the one that tells if the baby is a boy or a girl?"

Mamm shook her head, grinning a little. "*Nee*, but it's a girl. I was certain when Daniel was born that he would be a boy, and I was just as sure you were a girl. This baby is a girl." It was still hard to believe that *Mamm* was going to have a baby at her age. At least she wasn't throwing up anymore, and with each day that passed, she seemed more at peace about having a third child this late in life.

Annie picked up a seed catalog and flipped through it, unable to focus on anything besides Jacob. She wanted to hear more about his job. He'd told her it was a sales job and that he'd fill her in on more later, but he hadn't called, and she was starting to worry since he wasn't answering his cell phone. Maybe he'd already decided he wasn't coming back and didn't know how to tell her. She shrugged off the thought. Jacob hadn't been gone long enough to know what he wanted. Besides, she'd promised to give him the time he needed.

Amos had been in bed about an hour when Lena said, "You girls go to bed. You're both yawning, and it's getting late. And Charlotte, I know you are bound to still be very tired from your long night."

Charlotte nodded through another yawn, hoping she'd be able to sleep with everything on her mind, including the kiss she'd shared with Daniel.

Lena took off her prayer covering and scratched her head, the way Charlotte had seen her do a dozen times before in the privacy of Charlotte's apartment. Her head itched from her hair growing back in. Lena put the prayer covering back on. "We are *all* tired." She hugged Charlotte. "You are a light in our world, Charlotte. I know this is a tough time for you. But love bears all things."

"Do you think I'm doing the right thing, putting Janell in rehab? I mean, I don't know her. And she was awful to me . . . and—"

Lena held Charlotte's shoulders and looked into her eyes for a long time, then softly said, "'But I say unto you, Love your enemies, bless them that curse you, do good to them that hate you, and pray for them which despitefully use you, and persecute you.'" She smiled. "*Ya, mei maedel*, I think you are doing the right thing."

Lena went to her and Amos's bedroom and closed the door. A few minutes later, Charlotte followed Hannah upstairs with Buddy on her heels. "Well, hello, stranger." She turned around and picked Buddy up, scratching him behind the ears. "Decide you want to sleep with me tonight?"

Charlotte suspected Amos might have intentionally left Buddy outside of his room, thinking Charlotte might need her furry friend tonight. And he was right.

But despite everything that was happening, Charlotte and Hannah had barely gotten into their beds when Charlotte couldn't stand it anymore. "Daniel kissed me Saturday."

Hannah was upright instantly and gasped. She swung her legs off the bed, faced Charlotte, and brought a hand to her chest. "You're going to marry him!" Hannah turned up the flame on the lantern.

Charlotte tossed her covers back and sat up, facing Hannah. "Whoa there. It was just a kiss." Even Buddy seemed excited, wagging his tail with his tongue hanging out.

"How was it? Did you make plans to see each other again? I know you will be tending to your *mudder*, but is there room in your heart for him? Could you love him?"

Charlotte smiled at Hannah's enthusiasm—more like a teenager than a twentysomething woman. Charlotte didn't have answers to these questions. But as they giggled and speculated, Charlotte had a sense of belonging. And despite the problems that lay ahead, she felt stronger here. Family had a way of doing that to a person.

Monday morning during breakfast, Charlotte's name came up in conversation. Daniel filled his parents and Annie in on the latest happenings.

"Poor Charlotte," Annie said as she reached for a biscuit. "She's been through so much. Her breakup with her boyfriend and now this. But I'm so glad she's here now. She's lucky to have you, Daniel."

Daniel was the lucky one, if not a bit fearful. He scooped up a forkful of dippy eggs.

"Annie's right," *Mamm* said. "A person can never have too many friends."

Their mother couldn't have been any more obvious about her thoughts, emphasizing the word *friends*.

"I think Daniel and Charlotte are more than

friends." Annie giggled, but Daniel wanted to change the subject.

"Have you heard from Jacob?"

Annie paled, and Daniel wished he'd picked another topic. "*Nee*, and I'm very worried."

"He has a cell phone, *ya*?" Daniel asked with a mouthful.

"Sometimes he called me from his mobile phone and other times he called me from the phone in his fancy hotel room, but he said the man he was working for—Liam something—was getting him his own cell phone to use for work. He said he'd mail Charlotte's phone back to her."

Daed slammed a hand to the table, not hard—just enough to get everyone's attention. "These mobile phones go against everything we believe in. We are unequally yoked with the *Englisch*, and there is a reason for that." He pointed a finger at Daniel. "A fact you need to remember as you explore your new friendship with Charlotte. They are not like us."

Daniel suspected this was an argument he wouldn't win, and since he wasn't sure where things were headed with Charlotte, he decided to stay quiet until a time when he knew what he was fighting for.

Annie jumped when her cell phone vibrated in her apron pocket, and all eyes landed on their father, who was already shaking his head. His sister excused herself and ran for the stairs.

~

Jacob slouched into the chair in his hotel room and prepared himself for a lashing from Annie.

"Where have you been?" she hissed.

"I love you too," Jacob said in response to her clipped, accusatory voice. "I dropped the cell phone Charlotte gave me, so it stopped working. And I was having trouble making calls from the hotel room for some reason. Mr. Stone—well, he told me to call him Liam—got me a cell phone, but he said it's only for business, and I don't want to abuse his kindness. I can't stay on the phone long." Jacob glanced at the pile of new clothes on the bed. "He's been so nice to me, Annie."

"What exactly is your *business*, Jacob?"

He sighed. "Annie, can you let up with the attitude? Is this how it's going to be every time we talk?"

"*Nee, nee.* I'm sorry. I've just been worried since I haven't heard from you."

"I'm sorry I didn't call. I guess I need to get a cell phone for my personal calls."

"I don't understand why you can't use your work phone to call your family—and me."

Jacob stood up and paced the room in his new slacks and bare feet, running a hand through his much shorter blond hair. "I got a haircut. An *Englisch* haircut. Mr. Stone thought it was a *gut* idea." He glanced at his tattoo and flexed his muscle until the tattoo wiggled on his arm. Then he thanked God for his good fortune—the job and that he'd been able to hide the tattoo from Annie and his parents. Not an easy task.

"Well, if Mr. Stone thinks it's a *gut* idea, I'm sure it is."

Sometimes, when Annie got like this, Jacob wondered what he ever saw in her. But he knew. She was kind, loving, beautiful, and she would be a great mother someday. He was glad that wasn't a factor in their lives at the moment, though.

"What exactly is your job, Jacob?"

"Well, it's a real easy job. And Mr. Stone is paying me fifteen dollars an hour, plus letting me stay in this fancy hotel." Jacob chuckled. "Annie, I even have a driver to take me from place to place. Mr. Stone bought me some clothes too."

"What is the job?"

Jacob bit his tongue and reminded himself that Annie was the woman he loved. "Don't yell, Annie. I'm going to tell you. I told Mr. Stone that I had carried on my learning past the eighth grade, that I even knew calculus, so I'd hoped maybe my new job would have something to do with numbers, but it doesn't. I pretty much just ride from place to place with Evan."

"Doing what? And who is Evan?"

"Evan is a really big man with a dark tan. He speaks Spanish and *Englisch*. Very friendly fellow, not much older than me. Maybe thirty."

"Jacob, you're not even eighteen!"

"Well, I feel older, Annie. Quit hollering or I'm going to hang up."

"Jacob King, if you hang up on me, it will be the last time. I'm worried, that's all."

"Why can't you just be happy for me? You knew how worried I was about having enough money and finding a job. God is showering me with blessings! I have a fancy place to live, new clothes, and a great job."

"Well, I've about decided you're not going to tell me about this great new job. You drive from place to place doing what?"

"Here's what's so great . . . Mr. Stone's company delivers pharmaceuticals to people in the medical industry to distribute to doctors and hospitals." Jacob pulled back his shoulders, strutting around the room, knowing Annie wouldn't know what such big words meant. "Pharmaceuticals are medicines."

"I know what they are."

He narrowed his eyebrows, doubting that. "I take a suitcase to someone called a middleman. He gives me an envelope in return. Then the middleman delivers the medications to the doctors and hospitals. It's that easy." He scratched his head. "It's not challenging my mind very much, but I'm going to make a lot of money doing it. Mr. Stone said I might even be able to work my way up in the company. I work about six hours per day. There is a lot of driving around. But I don't mind. It gives me time to think."

"Why doesn't Mr. Stone deliver directly to the hospitals and doctors?"

Jacob clenched a fist and held it up, the way he'd seen people in the movies do when they had something important to say. "Here's the thing. Evan drives me to these houses, lots of them far away from Pittsburgh, and the houses are mansions—big fancy places with automatic gates, fountains, and long driveways . . . stuff like that. Sometimes Evan waits at the end of a long driveway while I walk the distance to the house. Mr. Stone said these are lifesaving medicines worth a lot of money. He can't take any chances that they might get in the hands of someone who might not use them the right way."

"Oh. What kind of lifesaving medicines? For cancer or something serious like that?"

"Exactly, Annie. I'm doing a very important job that saves lives."

Jacob waited for her to acknowledge the importance of his work, but Annie was quiet. She'd been through a lot, so Jacob decided not to tell her what was heaviest on his heart. That he was never going back to his old way of life.

Eighteen

Charlotte chewed on a fingernail as she sat across the desk from a woman named Glenda Ward, who was sharing an early evaluation of Janell. Not much happens at a hospital over the weekend, so it wasn't until Monday afternoon that Charlotte got some real information. Janell had spent the weekend licking her wounds, and the staff at the hospital said she was sleeping, clean, and comfortable for the past two days.

"Your mother is severely undernourished, jaundiced, and she's got a couple of cuts on her arms that we're treating. She's also anemic." Glenda had gray hair, short and above her ears, slightly spiked on the top. She was a heavyset woman with closely set blue eyes. Tapping a pencil on the desk, she said, "Janell talks out of her head sometimes but seems to make perfect sense other times. We have her sedated since we're trying to take care of her physical issues first." She paused. "I'm sure you are aware that your mother is addicted to methamphetamines."

Charlotte nodded.

"And she has been for a long time. At this point, it's hard to know how much that's affecting her mental state, but I suspect the doctors might find more than one diagnosis for Janell. She's already ripped the bandages off her arms twice. Has she, uh . . . been living with you?"

Charlotte had gone through all this on Friday when they checked Janell in, but she'd never spoken to Glenda before. *Isn't this information in the file?* "No. I haven't seen her in almost ten years."

Glenda's sharp eyes softened. "I see. Well, give us a couple more days to get some fluids and food in her, and she'll be evaluated by several more doctors, then we can see where we go from there."

Charlotte shifted uncomfortably in her chair. She'd done some research on this facility. Best she could tell, Janell would be forced out after a month unless she had insurance or a way to pay for her care. "My mother isn't a resident of Pennsylvania, and I just moved here, so I don't know how this works." Charlotte folded her hands in her lap, forcing herself to keep her fingers away from her mouth. "I—I guess I'm worried about being able to cover the costs."

Glenda smiled. "Don't worry. I need you to sign here as Janell's guardian, but the costs are being handled if there's a need for Janell to stay longer than a month, and I suspect that will be the case." She handed Charlotte a pen, clicking it once.

"What? By whom?"

"Amos King."

"What?" Charlotte asked again.

"I think some of this expense will be taken care of due to the nature of your mother's illness, but Mr. King said he would be picking up anything else."

Charlotte brought a hand to her overactive heart. "Do they have that kind of money?" *And why?*

Charlotte was speaking to herself, but Glenda chuckled. "I'm sure I wouldn't know, but many of the Amish around here are loaded. Think about it. No cars, most of them live on family properties, so no mortgage, no electric bill. They grow most of their own food and raise livestock. It doesn't cost them much to live." She paused. "They must think an awful lot of you to do this. Mr. King came by earlier today."

Charlotte scribbled her name on the guardianship paperwork, then stood up. "They're my family," she said in a shaky voice before she turned to leave.

"Charlotte . . ."

She turned around. Glenda was standing now. "Don't you want to see your mother? She's in a different room today."

Charlotte looked past the woman and out the window that faced a courtyard filled with colorful potted plants and two chairs. "Not today," she said before she turned and left.

Guilt nipped at her as she walked out of the building, but this entire thing with Janell was going to require baby steps, and today Charlotte had inched forward as much as she could.

~

When she got back to the King place, she saw Amos working the mules in the field. She hurried to the gate that separated the pasture from the front yard, then ran to where he was working. She bent at the waist, out of breath, as she waited for Amos to step down from the plow.

"Child, what is it?" Amos touched her on the arm, the first physical contact she'd had with him. "Tell me now. What is wrong? Is it Hannah? Lena?"

Charlotte straightened, and he dropped his hand to his side, his eyes wide and questioning.

"All I've wanted is for you to love me," she choked out. "To be the father I never had." She flung her arms in the air as tears streamed down her cheeks. "And most of the time, I don't even think you like me, and you surely haven't forgiven me. I appreciate you letting me use the truck, but I also know it was to help Annie. So . . . so I don't understand why you've gifted my mother with this random act of kindness, a woman you don't even know . . . who probably isn't worthy of your help any more than I'm worthy of your love."

Amos's eyes glazed over as he stared at her. "Is this what you think?" His voice was gravelly. He stepped closer to her, blinking his eyes a few times. After clearing his throat, he reached into his pocket and handed Charlotte an envelope that was folded in half. "This was in Jacob's room. Lena found it when she was stripping his bed. Jacob must have brought it from your apartment when he returned, unless you dropped it in there." He stroked his beard. "We read that you had been evicted from your apartment. I was only trying to help you with your mother since I supposed you had come upon hard times."

Charlotte cried harder. "Amos, I have no way to pay you back. I'm broke. My life is in shambles. My mother, who I haven't seen in ten years, has resurfaced, and I'm not sure how I feel about that." She bent at the waist again, trying to calm her breathing. "Some days I feel stronger, just being here with all of you, but Amos . . ." She tried to breathe. "I'm not just broke . . . I'm *broken*." She shook her head. "I don't know how to pay you back for this."

Amos opened his mouth to speak, but his bottom lip trembled. He cleared his throat again. "What you did . . ." He stopped speaking and stared at Charlotte. She held her breath and waited for Amos to write her off, to tell her the lies would not be forgiven, no matter her reasons, that he was only paying her mother's expenses because it was right in the eyes of the Lord.

"What you did"—he began again, his voice cracking—"for Lena." He hung his head, then finally looked at her with tears in his eyes. "I do not know how I could go on without my Lena. What you did for her . . . *I* can never repay."

Charlotte ran into his arms, and after a few moments, Amos embraced her too.

"I need you to forgive me," Charlotte said through her tears. "I need—"

"Hush, hush now, child." Amos kissed the top of Charlotte's head. "I was slower to forgive than the others, I admit. But I forgave you a long time ago. And what you did for Lena . . . you and her *Englisch* doctors . . . letting her stay with you, carting her to the hospital . . . such kindnesses I can't repay—" His voice broke again, and Charlotte hugged him tighter. "Helping your *mudder* is a small thing compared to what you did for Lena. It is easy to throw money at a problem. It's not as easy to do what you did. Lena told me about you holding her hair the times she was sick, about holding her hand each time she met with the doctors for more news about the cancer. There is no price tag for that."

"There will never be a need to repay me. I love you and Lena. And Hannah and Jacob. I love you all." Charlotte felt like she couldn't tell him enough.

"And we all love you, *maedel*."

In that moment, Charlotte wept as if purging herself of all the heavy baggage she'd been carting around.

"Charlotte . . ."

She stayed in his arms. *Don't stop hugging me just yet.*

"Your Father in heaven has not forsaken you, and He will guide your steps, but I would be honored to be your father during your time here on this earth."

Charlotte squeezed him tighter around the waist, not ready to let go.

Annie was fuming by Thursday afternoon. No call from Jacob since Monday. She'd called the hotel and asked them to ring his room, but the call never went through, despite her repeated attempts. She'd also redialed the number he had called her from on Monday, but no answer. She had her phone on vibrate in her apron pocket, which had become its permanent home, much to her father's dislike. She paced around the house alone. Her parents had hired a driver to take them to *Mamm*'s doctor appointment. This was her father's first visit to the *Englisch* doctor. The nurse had recommended he go, since they were doing an ultrasound to make sure everything was okay. Charlotte had offered to drive them to town, but *Daed* didn't think *Mamm* should ride in that "rickety clunker" as he'd called it.

Annie's only job for the day was to bake two loaves of bread and whip up a chicken casserole for supper, and she hadn't started either project. She stopped pacing when she heard a buggy coming up the driveway.

She peered through the front window. *Ugh.* She wasn't in the mood for Edna today.

"Hello, Edna," Annie said when she opened the door.

Edna held up a wicker basket covered with a dark blue towel. "I made way too many cookies for just John and me, and I remembered how much Daniel enjoys my peanut butter cookies."

"*Danki*, do you want to come in for a while? I'm the only one home." *Please say no.* Annie was much too distracted about Jacob, she hadn't done her chores, and Edna's visits were always a fishing trip. Annie wondered what information Edna was in search of today. The woman had tried to be Annie's best friend when she was dating Daniel.

"*Ya*, that would be nice. It gets lonely at our farm when John is at work." Edna handed the basket to Annie, then they went to the kitchen. Annie offered Edna some coffee and put out a cookie for each of them before they sat down.

"Maybe it's time to start a family," Annie said before taking a bite.

Edna bit into her cookie but didn't look at Annie. "*Ya, ya.*" After she'd taken a sip of coffee, she said, "So I hear Charlotte is in town again. I hope it's not to torment the Kings again." She shook her head.

Annie's mood was just bad enough to unload on Edna if the woman wasn't careful. "The Kings love Charlotte. And I'm pretty sure something is going on between Daniel and Charlotte." Annie smiled before taking another bite of the cookie.

"That seems unlikely. Charlotte isn't Daniel's type."

"Why not? She's beautiful and smart."

Edna put her cookie down on the napkin. "She's not Amish, for starters. And have you forgotten all the lies she told when she was pretending to be Amish? She's not a *gut* person."

"Charlotte is a great person, and we've all forgiven her for that. What she did was wrong, but she wanted to know why her brother ended his life." She was fueling Edna's emotions, but Edna had hurt Daniel when she stopped dating him, and that hadn't sat well with Annie.

Edna shook her head. "I don't trust her."

Annie shoved in the last bite of her cookie. *And I don't trust you.* "*Ach*, well . . . you'll have plenty of opportunities to get to know her better. She's been living with the Kings, but she's decided not to sell Ethan's house. Instead, she's going to live there, so this is truly a permanent arrangement for her."

Edna choked on her bite of cookie and covered her mouth.

It was a week later before Charlotte was ready to visit Janell. She parked Big Red, which she'd grown accustomed to driving, and baby-stepped all the way to the entrance of the rehabilitation center. After she'd verified what room Janell was in, she walked the long hallway, pausing at room 245 before she walked in. Her mother was lightly snoring. Charlotte walked to the edge of the bed and stared at her. With the exception of being clean, Janell didn't look much different from when Charlotte found her. Maybe a little more color in her face, but she still had dark circles underneath her eyes, and the sores on her face looked red and irritated.

Charlotte took a step backward and sat in a nearby chair, wondering if anyone in Janell's life was looking for her. *Does she have any friends, anyone who cares what happens to her?* Charlotte would have picked up an animal on the side of the street and taken it to a vet if need be. This felt shamefully the same to her. She was having trouble finding compassion amid all the dark memories that had bubbled to the surface. But this woman had given birth to her. It was all in God's plan. Charlotte was trying, and for now, that was all she could do.

Janell opened her eyes and blinked them into focus. "I wondered if you'd come." She spit the words at Charlotte while keeping her face void of any expression.

"Well, I did."

"You didn't have to. I did without you for ten years, so I reckon I could keep on doing it." She reached for a glass of water and moved the straw to her mouth.

Janell wasn't slurring her words like she was overmedicated or anything. She was just plain mean. "Uh, you say that like it's my fault."

Janell set the glass of water on the tray by her hospital bed. "Well, ain't it?"

Charlotte tapped her foot against the tile floor, slow at first, then faster, as if she was winding herself up to sprint from the room when the time came. "Sure, Janell. I guess it was my fault." Charlotte felt childish for mocking her mother's attitude, but shouldn't there be some tiny bit of appreciation?

"Don't you get smart with me, young lady." Janell pressed what was left of her teeth together, sneering at Charlotte.

"Everything okay in here?" A nurse walked into the room, raised an eyebrow, and walked to the side of the bed. She looked about Janell's age. "Is this the daughter you were talking about?" The woman extended her hand to Charlotte. "I'm Lorraine. Janell told me she had a daughter that might be visiting."

Charlotte smiled. "Nice to meet you."

Janell grunted and rolled her eyes. "That ain't her. That ain't the daughter I was talking about."

Charlotte frowned as she shook her head and locked

eyes with Lorraine. "I'm Charlotte, and I'm the only daughter she has." She paused, then leaned toward the nurse and whispered, "Is she medicated?" Even though her words weren't slurred, she wasn't making a lot of sense.

Lorraine glanced at Janell, then back at Charlotte. "No, she's not on much medication. We've been weaning her off of everything."

"That explains the meanness," she said under her breath. It just slipped out, and she wished Lorraine hadn't heard, but it was too late.

Janell grunted loudly. "I told you! What did I tell you, Nurse Lorraine? I said I had one nice daughter and one mean daughter." She pointed to Charlotte. "And this is the mean one. I felt better when I was staying in Ethan's house."

"Janell, we talked about all this," Lorraine said. "You felt better before because of the drugs, but you don't need drugs to feel good. We're going to have you feeling better soon without all those toxins in your body."

Charlotte was confused. Janell seemed to be half in reality, half in some fantasy land. "Anyway, I just stopped by to see how you were doing. I've seen, so I'll go." She turned to Lorraine. "Good luck."

She was almost out the door when Janell yelled, "My other daughter will come to see me."

"That's good," Charlotte said over her shoulder. "Maybe you'll be nicer to her."

Lorraine caught Charlotte before she got too far down the hallway, tears already building. "Hon—"

Charlotte stopped but didn't look at the woman.

"She's a drug addict, and she's trying to wean off some bad stuff that she's been doing for a very long time. Maybe don't take everything she says to heart."

Charlotte looked at Lorraine. "I don't know how to take it any other way. She's no different than she was." She reached inside her purse, dug around for her keys, and realized she didn't have them. "Ugh. I must have left my keys in her room."

"I'd offer to go get them for you, but that's me they're paging." She held up one finger and an ear toward the ceiling. "*Lorraine, station six.*" Waving, she hurried down the hallway, and Charlotte slowly marched back to room 245, thinking she liked Janell better when she was drugged out and not making sense.

"I forgot my keys," she said as she shuffled to where she spotted them on the floor by the chair.

"You hooked up with that Amish fellow that was with you?" Janell was sitting up in bed now, more than before. "Them are some bad people, those weirdos."

Walk away, don't engage, walk away. Charlotte took a deep breath. "No, I am not hooked up with that Amish man. He is a friend. And the Amish people are not weirdos."

"Maybe you're right." Janell frowned. "I don't know."

Charlotte's need to stay and defend her Amish

friends was strong, but her need to leave was stronger. "Bye, Janell."

"You know it was an Amish person that snatched Dianda from my arms that day. That horrible woman had no regard for my feelings at all. That awful woman in her Amish getup took you into the store while someone else carried Ethan off kicking and screaming in another direction, peeling their tires as they left. I didn't get you and Ethan back for two years, but I never did get my baby girl back."

Charlotte fell into the chair as she dropped her purse beside her and grabbed her chest. *The secret I'm keeping from myself.* She squeezed her eyes closed as foggy memories slammed into her with the strength and destruction of hurricane winds about to blow a person into oblivion.

"What? You don't remember that woman snatching you in your little purple dress and dragging you away? You couldn't have been more than three or four, Ethan maybe five or six. We never spoke about Dianda, our sweet little Andy, as we called her."

Yes, you did. As Charlotte struggled to stay in the chair, hearing the name Dianda was triggering all kinds of partial memories that wouldn't come together. She could vaguely recall Ethan asking about Dianda—and getting knocked upside the head for doing so. Time must have been kind to them both and stripped them of the memories.

"Where is she now, Dianda?" Charlotte asked in barely a whisper, the knot in her throat growing so much that Charlotte was sure it was going to cut off her air supply.

"Beats me." Janell shrugged.

"Then why . . ." Charlotte drew in a long breath and blew it out slowly. "Then why in the world would you think she would show up here for a visit?"

Janell's bottom lip trembled, and she tried several times to speak before she finally said, "She won't." She half smiled as tears poured down her face. "But in my mind, she doesn't know me." She paused as she blinked back more tears. "If she doesn't know me, maybe she can love me. Even though I gave her away."

Charlotte stared at this woman who birthed her, whose bloodline she shared, and she had no words. She stood up and slowly walked out of the room, but she hadn't gotten far when she broke into a run. And she ran until she found the chapel.

It was a week later before Charlotte was ready to face the world, including Daniel. She'd spoken to him on the phone, but she'd mostly stayed in the comfort of her family's arms; Hannah, Lena, Amos, and God the Father. Hannah read to Charlotte from the Bible each evening, often elaborating on each verse and what it meant to her. Lena had made sure Charlotte had an unlimited amount of buttered bread and a shoulder to cry on that was always nearby. Amos was reserved, but Charlotte felt his fatherly love in the little things he did for her—like making sure Big Red was safe to drive. He'd installed a rearview mirror and regularly checked the fluids. God the Father had shown her how to forgive. Charlotte had been forgiven time and time again, and now it was her turn to forgive her parents, once and for all, to release that burden to Him.

"Are you sure you're ready to move? It hasn't been that long." Hannah swiped at her eyes, and Charlotte pulled her into a hug.

"It's not like I'm going back to Texas. I'm just moving a few miles away." She kissed Hannah on the cheek, then made her way to Lena. "I love you," she whispered.

And last but never least, she hugged Amos, who was reluctant at first, but he hugged her back. "Give me a call sometimes," he said, which made everyone laugh since Amos didn't approve of all the cell phone usage.

Then she leaned down and scooped up Buddy. "You ready to go, little guy?" She nuzzled his face, but when she saw the forlorn expression on Amos's face, almost as if he might cry, she did the most unselfish thing she could think of as repayment for all Amos had done for her. She handed him Buddy. "Here."

Amos stood holding the dog with his arms straight out. "What? What are you doing?"

Don't cry, don't cry. "I'm going to be busy, Amos, and trying to save my money. I thought you could take care of Buddy now." She thought about her mother giving away Dianda, and almost snatched Buddy back. But this wasn't the same thing. Amos finally brought the dog to his chest and smiled. Jacob was gone, at least for now. Hannah would leave in the fall when she married Isaac. The house would seem quiet to Amos and Lena.

Charlotte threw her purse in the passenger seat of Big Red, climbed in, and waved to her family.

Daniel was standing in the front yard of Ethan's house when Charlotte pulled in. When she hadn't felt strong enough to share details with Daniel, Hannah had briefed him on everything as it happened. He held out his arms to her, and Charlotte fell into his embrace.

"Thank you for coming." She raised her chin and smiled. Today was a day for new beginnings, and she refused to let sadness consume her anymore. God the Father was walking beside her, and to let fear and worry overtake her would be saying she didn't have faith in His plan for her.

Daniel walked to the porch steps to sit down and motioned for her to do the same. Charlotte looked out over the fields filled with spring blooms, as the sun shone brightly on a day that represented a new phase in Charlotte's life. Daniel was quiet.

"You know, I figured Janell would have walked out of rehab by now, but I call every day, and she's still there."

"But you haven't seen her again?"

Charlotte was quiet for a few moments. "No. I haven't. Glenda, the lady that works there, said Janell asks about me every day, but . . ." She shrugged. "I don't know. I've spent a large part of my life hating my mother, so it's hard to just turn that off. I've forgiven her and my father, but Janell is hard to be around."

Daniel took off his hat and set it on his lap. Then he looked at her and smiled. "I saw something more than hate when you found your mother. It might not be an emotion you connect to her, but there was love in your heart too."

Since Janell had shown up, memories were flooding Charlotte's mind, events that she'd pushed back for years. She recalled the first time Child Protective Services had showed up at their house, and she'd had the tiniest recollection of a baby. "How could I love her? She was awful to me and my brother. And she apparently gave away a baby sister I didn't know I had." The social worker that was assigned to Charlotte's mother at the facility had contacted Charlotte. The woman—Patricia—suggested Charlotte might like to see a counselor, an offer Charlotte had taken her up on. Her first appointment was next week.

"We don't choose how we feel. It just is what it is."

"So here we are, at my new home." Charlotte took in her surroundings, the empty flower beds that she planned to fill with color, and . . . She gasped when her eyes landed where Ethan's tree used to be. There wasn't so much as a stump left. She stood up and brought both her hands to her chest. "The tree. It's gone."

"You said you hated that tree." Daniel stood up and put a hand on her shoulder. "And part of it was, um . . . diseased. So it never would have been whole again or healthy. It would have only gotten worse. I had someone chop it down."

Charlotte wrapped her hands around his neck. "Thank you."

"You're welcome." Daniel motioned for her to follow him inside as he took a key from his pocket, then unlocked the door. He pushed open the door so she could go in first. "It's warm in here without electricity and the air-conditioning you're used to, but I installed several battery-operated fans throughout the house and made sure all the windows had good screens."

Charlotte smiled as she crossed the living room, then went to the bedroom, then the kitchen. She met up with him back in the living room. Every single room in the house had been painted.

"You said beadboard white, pastels on the upper half of the walls, right? I didn't know for sure what colors you might like, but we all painted in colors we wished we had in our houses." He chuckled. "Isaac painted the kitchen a light yellow. Hannah and Lena came by after delivering food to some shut-ins, and they painted the living room this pale blue." Daniel's face turned a light shade of red.

"I painted your bedroom a soft, light green. If you dislike these colors, I'll help you redo them."

Charlotte went from room to room again. She wondered if there would ever come a day when she didn't feel like crying for one reason or another. "This overwhelms me. I love every color. I—" She almost said it. But there was still one thing hanging between them. "Daniel . . . I have something that I've been hiding from you. I don't want it between us for one more second." She took a breath and lowered her head. "I was evicted from my apartment. That's why I moved here."

He sighed, the expression on his face full of love. "*Ya*, I know. Jacob found your eviction notice before he left your apartment, and he told Annie." He smiled. "I don't care why you came here. I'm just glad you're here."

Charlotte looked around the house again. "I cannot believe you, Isaac, Lena, and Hannah got this house painted so quickly. I just can't believe it . . ."

"*Ach*, well . . . we had help. We were just the chiefs directing the Indians. The same Indians that will be helping us today." Daniel motioned for her to follow him outside, then he pointed to the road, at the long line of buggies turning onto the road that led to Charlotte's house. "They are bringing all of your things. When you were sleeping day before yesterday, Isaac and others loaded everything from the basement into buggies we usually use to cart our benches for worship service."

She put a hand over her mouth and eased herself

down onto the porch step again. "Do I even know all of these people?"

Daniel sat down beside her, both of them watching the dozens of buggies heading their way. "I don't know. Hannah is probably the head chief." He laughed. "She has a group coming to clean, another one bringing food, and Isaac has some men coming to help repair the fence in the backyard, even though you'd originally told him not to worry about it. And we will have plenty of folks to unload and get your furniture arranged."

They were quiet as they waited for the others. But Charlotte recalled something she'd asked God for awhile back. "I prayed that whoever ended up in this house would have peace and happiness." She stood up and turned to Daniel. "How could I have known I was praying for myself?"

"God is *gut*," Daniel said softly.

Charlotte reached for Daniel's hand, not having the words to communicate what was in her heart. He squeezed her hand three times, and she smiled.

"Do you know what that means, when you squeeze someone's hand three times?" Charlotte asked him.

"*Ya*, I do. Do you?"

She squeezed his hand back the same amount of times. "I sure do."

They both smiled and slowly walked across the yard, hand in hand, ready to greet the people who'd come to help Charlotte start her new life.

Epilogue

Dear Ethan,

I'm sorry I haven't written lately. Three months ago, I decided to permanently move to Lancaster County. I'm living in your little blue house, so I enjoy being close to my family—Hannah, Lena, and Amos. I am spending a lot of time with Daniel Byler, but we've agreed to take things slow since we've both been hurt in the past. And I'm not Amish, so that is reason enough not to rush anything. I'm seeing a therapist again, working through some of my own issues. I want to feel whole again before I commit to sharing my life with anyone.

I didn't have electricity put in your house, so in many ways, I live like my Amish friends. Although I haven't shed my worldly ways entirely, I've given up makeup and don't have a way to blow-dry my hair, so I guess that's a start. I don't really miss television, but I do miss air-conditioning during these hot summer months. And it's hard to imagine not having a vehicle, so that's a luxury I hang on to. Although there are those who might not consider Big Red luxurious, I've grown rather attached to my gift from Amos. Who knows what the future holds—only God. For now, I try to keep things simple.

Ethan, Janell showed up here in Lancaster County. I couldn't believe it. Somehow, the police tracked her down and notified her about your death. From there, she did some digging around until she found out where you'd lived—and died. I am doing the best I can to help her get well. Our mother had more problems than either of us were aware of as children. She is in a psychiatric hospital that also deals with drug addiction. She still has a long way to go, but she is making progress. I visit her once a week. That's about all I can handle right now. With each day, Janell seems to be shedding some of the anger, but she also cries a lot. Some weeks she seems happy to see me, and other times she's as mean as I remember her.

The haunting memories hover around me, and sometimes I feel like a fish caught in a net of despair, but it passes, and as quickly as I'm trapped—I find my way free again. Hopefully, someday I'll be free from the nightmares altogether.

Janell told me that our father is dead. I'm working through my feelings about that with my therapist, but it's slow going. I rely just as much on prayer as I do on my therapist when it comes to forgiving our parents. I've forgiven them, but I am also struggling to shed my anger toward them.

Ethan, we have a sister. Maybe you have a vague recollection of her since you are older than me. Maybe you can see her from your heavenly home. Is she safe? Is she well? Her name is Dianda Rochelle Dolinsky . . . Dianda. I will look for her when I feel stronger. And I feel stronger every day, determined to be the master of my own destiny, through God's guidance.

I am working for a local newspaper doing some proofing and editing work. I finally came to the conclusion that I just don't have the self-discipline to work for myself. I'm distracted too easily, and I also just wasn't getting as much work sent my way. The job at the newspaper is steady income, and I'm slowly getting back on my feet financially.

Hannah and Isaac will be married soon, but things have changed for Jacob and Annie. I can tell that Jacob's choices are causing a lot of pain for his parents and sister, but Lena, Amos, and Hannah continue to hold out hope that Jacob will leave the *Englisch* world and come back to them. Annie is taking his absence the hardest, and she hears less and less from Jacob with each passing week. We all pray that he stays safe and well.

It's amazing how much comfort and support family can bring. I'll never have that with Janell, but I continue to try to make room for our mother in my heart. I can't bring myself to call her Mom, and she doesn't say anything when I call her Janell.

I'll keep writing to you, as my previous therapist suggested awhile back. Even though you aren't physically in this world, I feel your presence here in the peacefulness of a place I now call home.

Rest in peace, my beloved brother.

All my love,
Char

Discussion Questions

1. In the beginning of the story, we learn that Charlotte repeatedly checked Ryan's text messages based on her suspicions that he was cheating on her. Ultimately, she finds out that Ryan *was* cheating on her. Was it still wrong for her to check his text messages, or did you think her actions were justified?
2. Edna isn't portrayed as a very nice character in the story. But are you able to dig deeper and ponder what prompts her to seek love in all the wrong places, so to speak? Was Daniel correct when he tells Charlotte that Edna seems to be searching for more love than is humanly possible?

3. Annie and Jacob are both a bit flighty and unsure about what they want. Were you happy that Annie wasn't pregnant, or were you disappointed? Do you think that the couple's fate would have been sealed if Annie had really been pregnant? What would they have both ultimately chosen if that had been the case?
4. Like the rest of us, Charlotte isn't perfect. She is striving to get her life in order, to be the best person she can be, and to take care of her mother despite her upbringing. What are some other examples of Charlotte's spiritual growth?
5. Jacob ultimately chooses not to go back to Lancaster County, and it's fairly obvious that he is heading down a path that might not be best suited for him. What do you think will happen? If you could create an alternate ending for Jacob's thread in the story, what would it be? Or would it be the same, knowing that God leads us down wrong paths for a reason sometimes because it's the only route to the right path?
6. Daniel is first attracted to Charlotte because she's pretty. He recognized that outer beauty is never enough. What characteristic does Daniel notice about Charlotte early on that makes her attractive to him, not just on the outside?

Acknowledgments

I wait until my final reading on a project before I choose who the book will be dedicated to. It seems like God always lays the perfect person on my heart during that part of the process. In *Love Bears All Things*, Amos King is a quiet and well-respected man, and Charlotte longs for his fatherly love. Even her finicky dog—Buddy—takes a liking to Amos. Terry Newcomer is like a father on earth to me since my own father is singing with the angels. He's also my dear friend. There are many parallels with Terry and Amos. It's an honor to dedicate this book to Terry Newcomer, as fine a man as I've ever known.

I've been blessed abundantly with a fabulous husband, great friends, and an awesome family. Much thanks and love goes out to all of you.

To my wonderful assistant/marketing coordinator—Janet Murphy—thank you for being my voice of reason and for keeping me organized and sane, which I know is not always an easy task. You are appreciated and loved more than words can say.

Natasha Kern, I'll never run out of good things to say about you. My agent. My friend. You always go above and beyond in every aspect of managing my career, but what touches my heart so much is the way you are always available and nurturing when it's my personal life that needs managing. Love you tons.

To my editor Becky Philpott and all the folks at HarperCollins Christian Fiction, thank you for always believing in me and for the many opportunities you've provided me with over the years. I'm blessed to have such a dedicated team, and I'm thankful for each and every one of you.

Natalie Hanemann, I'm so thankful to have you on my team, but even more grateful for the friendship we share. You've been on this ride with me from the beginning, and I'm blessed to have you in my life, both professionally and personally. Love you, sweet friend.

And Dear God . . . Thank you again for providing me with another story that I hope entertains readers and glorifies You. *I can do all things through Christ who strengthens me.*

About the Author

Beth Wiseman is the award-winning and bestselling author of the Daughters of the Promise, Land of Canaan, and Amish Secrets series. While she is best known for her Amish novels, Beth has also written contemporary novels including *Need You Now*, *The House that Love Built*, and *The Promise*.

You can read the first chapter of all of Beth's
books at www.bethwiseman.com.
Facebook: Fans of Beth Wiseman
Twitter: @bethwiseman

9781401685942-B

What would cause the Amish to move to Colorado, leaving family and friends behind?

The Land of Canaan Series

Also available in e-book formats

9781401685942-A